The Skipper
& the *Eagle*

The *Eagle* in a good breeze.

The Skipper
& the *Eagle*

by
Capt. Gordon McGowan

Foreword by Captain Alan Villiers
Introduction by Peter Stanford
Afterword by Capt. Robert J. Papp, Jr., USCG

SEA HISTORY PRESS
NATIONAL MARITIME HISTORICAL SOCIETY
PEEKSKILL, NEW YORK

The original edition of *The Skipper and the Eagle* was published in 1960 by D. Van Nostrand Company (Canada), Ltd. The Introduction, Afterword and Appendices are new with this edition, as are the photographs that follow the Afterword.

The National Maritime Historical Society is indebted to the Patrons of this book for providing the funding for its publication, and to Mr. Russell Drumm of Montauk, New York, a dedicated scholar of the *Eagle*'s history, for his assistance. And we are indebted to Mr. Edward Lowe of North Stonington, Connecticut, and Mr. Emil Babich of Oak Ridge, New Jersey, for their help providing information about the voyage in which they were participating US Coast Guard crew.

Copyright © 1998 by
National Maritime Historical Society
5 John Walsh Boulevard
Peekskill, New York 10566

Library of Congress Catalogue Card # 60-9033
ISBN 0-930248-09-0

Edited by Norma Stanford
Printed in Canada

NATIONAL MARITIME HISTORICAL SOCIETY
5 JOHN WALSH BOULEVARD, PEEKSKILL, NEW YORK 10566

PATRONS

Publication of this new augmented edition is made possible by the generous contributions of

GUY E. C. MAITLAND

and

HOWARD SLOTNICK

Contents

Introduction

The United States Coast Guard Cutter *Eagle* has seen the worst of times and the best of times. Launched in 1936 as the *Horst Wessel*, from the Blohm & Voss shipyard in Hamburg, the same yard that built the mighty German battleship *Bismarck* (which sank the famed British battlecruiser *Hood*, before she herself was hunted down and destroyed), the graceful barque had only a few years of service training seamen under sail for the Kriegsmarine before World War II broke out in 1939. Her part in the war ended, as the author of this authentic narrative describes, grounded and canted over at a drunken angle in the bombed-out ruins of the German port of Bremerhaven.

Captain McGowan gives his first-hand account of how Americans and Germans learned to pull together for the ship, sailing her across the Atlantic as a war prize to her new home in the United States. The voyage was made in 1946, when the *Eagle* was just ten years old. She has reeled off more than fifty years of sailing since then, in voyages ranging from Leningrad (now St. Petersburg), with our NMHS members Walter Cronkite and Howard Slotnick aboard, to Sydney, Australia, on the other side of the world. This half century has been sailed in peace, doing work of the most important kind: training young Americans in the disciplines of seafaring— hard-won disciplines of initiative, cooperation and respect that translate to every condition and every walk of life.

In his Afterword written for this new edition of McGowan's book, Captain Bob Papp, the present commander of the *Eagle*, speaks to us eloquently of that learning experience as he has led it aboard the ship and seen its results in action.

Sometimes civilians sail aboard the *Eagle*, when her regular duties training officers for the US Coast Guard permit. On one such occasion years ago, in June 1967, I was one of those fortunate persons. This came about because the *Eagle* had come in on a visit to the newly established South Street Seaport Museum, which I then served as president. I embarked from South Street for a five-day offshore exercise.

And how completely, as we made sail standing out to sea, the clustering concerns of the fledgling museum were swept from my head! Handling sail aloft was a wonderful change from making phone calls and strained visits to downtown offices to collect dollars to meet the costs of the growing museum. At sea we had our share of rain and calms, but under Captain Carkeek and his able executive officer "Hap" Paulsen the ship and her people were constantly worked and constantly learning. It was Hap Paulsen who ordered me to read Felix Riesenberg's *Standard Seamanship*, a fine book salted with the learning of his experience before the mast in a Cape Horn voyage in the Downeaster *A.J. Fuller* just before 1900.

What glorious reading! Riesenberg made sense of all the traditional commands. His description of making ready to bring the ship about is a classic which I copied into my journal, now open before me as I write: *"Hands about ship" meant all hands, and the cook at the fore sheet, a time-honored station filled by the Celestial with all the importance in the world.*

Riesenberg made you see the scenes on deck, and the few bits I couldn't get clear were soon straightened out for me by Captain Carkeek. He wanted every man Jack and woman aboard that ship to know the ways of the sea!

Not everyone can sail aboard the *Eagle*. But we can all share in her story, which shines like a beacon in a world confused by too much noisy information and too little sense of purpose and direction. A sailing ship confers these gifts. I have seen this happen time and again in my work for the

National Maritime Historical Society, where we seek out the ageless truths of seafaring. And of no ship is this more true than the *Eagle*, aboard which, as Captain Papp points out, you'll meet some of the finest citizens this country can produce.

When the *Eagle* put her lines ashore again in South Street in that distant June thirty-one years ago, my children came aboard with the visiting public, and I remember my own sense of positive elation as they asked questions about the thickets of rigging all about them and the great coils of line hanging from the pinrails, ready to spread canvas to the free winds that roam the oceans—and as they simply gazed up in speechless wonder at the masts which seem so much taller than any building ashore.

Today the *Eagle* is known around the world as "America's Tall Ship." She leads the world's sail training ships when they visit our shores in Operation Sail, and she carries the best kind of message when she sails to foreign shores. Long may she course the world's oceans and inspire our young and the young at heart with the challenge and wonder of seafaring under sail!

PETER STANFORD
President
National Maritime Historical Society

Preface

There is a tall white ship moored on the Thames River in New London, Connecticut—a three-masted bark. Every year in the first week of June, U. S. Coast Guard cadets swarm aboard this "antique" and set forth on a foreign cruise.

This proud ship once flew the swastika of Nazi Germany. Here is the story of her first voyage under the Stars and Stripes.

To Readers uninitiated in sea lore:

TRAVELING LIZARDS, KNIGHTHEADS, SPRITS'LS, CROJICKS, BUMKINS, PARRALS, HOUNDS, CLUE GARNETS, and FUTTOCKS are all respectable nautical terms, but none of them will be found in this book beyond this page.

The nautical terms which were used are considered necessary for the telling, and where it appeared that they might seem esoteric to the landsman an attempt has been made to explain them.

To my Shipmates:

You know that I did not consult you in the writing of this book. No two witnesses in a courtroom tell exactly the same story without there being collusion involved. Your remembrance of this episode may disagree with mine. I have set down the facts as I remember them.

GORDON MCGOWAN

Foreword

The United States Coast Guard is a unique and magnificent Service. In America, its ubiquitous efficiency is taken for granted, and the manifold tasks of its extraordinary fleet of fifty different types of vessel make the headlines only when they chance to be more than usually sensational, or stirring. The Coast Guard patrols, rescues, guards, keeps inland waters ice-free and oceans ice-patrolled; maintains aids to navigation, long-range and short, far and near; superintends the seaworthiness of American shipping and the serviceability of American ports. Its carefully trained and rigorously selected personnel include skilled naval architects, examiners of masters and mates, surveyors of harbors and of ships, skilled ice-pilots and airplane pilots too, trained lawyers experienced in matters of seafaring law. Its seamen are first-class and its pilots, sea and air, outstanding. In the U.S.A., I say, it is taken for granted, like so much else; but the rest of the maritime world doffs its seafaring cap in homage and salutation. In Europe, a coastguard is apt to be some ancient naval pensioner, with a telescope under one arm, ambling up a cliff or to some lookout-post in time of gale. He can give a good account of himself, too, when it comes to rescue operations. But his service is a limited one, and the manifold duties undertaken for the people of the United States by their Coast Guard are entrusted in Britain, to a dozen different government departments—Trinity House, the Board of Trade, Sundry departments of the Ministry of Transport, the Royal National Lifeboat Institute, and the Royal Navy.

When there was a big barque available in Germany at the end of the second world war in part reparations, it did not surprise me that the U.S. Coast Guard accepted her. There was little competition. Most sea services lacked either the foresight to use such a ship or the know-how to sail her, if they had her, or both. But the Coast Guard is a sail-trained service from its origins in Alexander Hamilton's day, and it has always done its best to maintain that excellent tradition. It chartered the ship *Danmark* through the war years to keep its skill. And so, it had use for such a ship as the *Horst Wessel,* and it knew what to do with her. She was a stout barque, almost new as square-riggers go, with strong rigging and a strong motor as well. She had some war damage, but that could be put right. She was the perfect seagoing school-ship for attachment to the C. G. Academy, at New London, just right in size, capacity, and accommodations. She still had a nucleus of her original German crew to help to get her over. She had defects, of course, but these could all be put right, and were. The *Horst Wessel* had the great good fortune to have Captain Gordon McGowan appointed to her as her first American commanding officer—a Coast Guard man, Coast Guard trained. He took her over, made her over, brought her over. There were difficulties, and he overcame them. There were troubles, and he sailed through them. There were problems, and he solved them.

Gordon McGowan was the first in a distinguished line of Coast Guard commanders of the barque *Eagle* ex—*Horst Wessel*—Miles Imlay, Carl Olsen, Carl Bowman, Karl Zittel. Between them they have been sailing the big barque now for more than a dozen years, without accident, without fuss—just, indeed, as one would expect them to do. And I hope they and their like will go on sailing her for the next fifty. She does a good job, and she serves a splendid Service.

The Germans? They replaced the *Horst Wessel* with a fine new barque when they could—the *Gorch Foch,* built by Blohm and Voss, and now the German Navy's new sailing school-ship. And they get on very quietly and efficiently with sailing her, too.

ALAN VILLIERS

Oxford, England.
October 26, 1959

List of Illustrations

Chapter I

"Let fall!"

Gripping a jackstay with one hand and shoving mightily with the other, the men on the yards released the sails and they dropped into the clews, where they lay half unfurled ready to be set taut. Above the chugging of the diesel exhaust, the chattering of the crew sounded like the twittering of migrating blackbirds. Broken fragments of sentences intermingled:

"Hey, give me a hand on this line!"

"Vass iss loss?"

"Get off my foot, you damn fool."

"Gott fer dammen!"

"Put your weight on the footropes; my part is sagging."

"Fertsaiung."

"I'll race you down the backstays. Last one on deck's a rotten egg!"

They sidestepped along the footropes toward the masts, and came swarming down to the deck from their sail stations. The excitement was infectious. Our first setting of sail on the broad ocean, with over five thousand miles of voyage ahead of us! The auxiliary engine fuel tanks carried just enough diesel oil to get in and out of harbors and through an occasional patch of calm weather. This ship was built primarily to sail, and sail we must.

With the sails loosed, setting taut was next in the order of business. The ship hummed with activity as tacks and sheets were set down into place, while yards were being hoisted and wrinkles began to disappear from the billowing canvas. I rang "Stop" on the engine telegraph and 'phoned

1

the engine room to disengage the propeller clutch. As the noise of the diesel died away, a new soft sound took its place —the song of the breeze in the rigging.

This sudden new peace was short-lived. As we picked up speed and started to adjust the braces and set taut on a line here, slack a line there, the all-new running rigging taught me a hard lesson in seamanship. The line twisted and kinked in a fiendish fashion. Tacks and sheets were hopelessly snarled. In no time at all we were practically helpless.

Before we could get the slack out of some of our new lines they began to squirm as if alive, and coiled themselves into a confusion of rat's nests and animated knots. Every tackle in sight was immobile, the blocks widely separated by twisted and fouled lines. Stress on new line had done us dirt. The only way out was to unreeve and re-reeve the gear until the twists and rat's nests could be worked out. Line by line we dismantled and reassembled. I made a solemn resolution that never again would I renew rigging unnecessarily.

Earlier, in Bremerhaven, the discovery of a warehouse full of new Manila line had been considered a lucky break and I had gone hog wild in renewing running rigging. Our proud start at sailing this handsome ship was a disgraceful mess. A quick squall right at this point would bring real trouble. Running new line into the rigging of a sailing ship is like putting on a new pair of shoes. This tightness and unyielding stiffness should have been foreseen. To a Cape Horn square-riggerman this would have been an elementary truism, but to her present crew the unreasonable behavior of the new gear aloft was a rude shock and a bitter disappointment. Fortunately, the weather was holding good; otherwise we would be in serious trouble now.

Six months ago I had received my orders:

"ON OR ABOUT 18 JANUARY 1946 PROCEED BY AIR TO LONDON ENGLAND AND REPORT TO COMNAVEU FOR FURTHER ASSIGNMENT AS PROSPECTIVE COMMANDING OFFICER OF THE COAST GUARD CUTTER EAGLE NOW THE GERMAN EX-NAVAL SHIP HORST WESSEL AT THE US NAVAL ADVANCE BASE WESER RIVER BREMERHAVEN GERMANY."

After teaching seamanship at the Coast Guard Academy in New London a little over three years, I was due for sea duty. For that I was fully prepared, but not for this turn of events. A transfer is like death in the family; it often comes as no surprise, but seldom without a shock.

Some weeks before, the Superintendent of the Academy. had got wind of the dividing up of the German fleet, and he knew that among the prizes of war there was a three-masted bark. When he applied for the vessel, he touched off a big debate in the service, a debate which recurs from time to time. The pros favored going back to fundamentals in sail training in giving the young cadets their introduction to the sea; the cons maintaining that life is too short in these technical times to waste any of the precious four years of the Academy course on antiquity. My orders were proof that our Superintendent, and the pros, had prevailed.

Any seaman worth his salt would be happy at the idea of getting such a unique assignment. Although I was a steam sailor and did not pretend to be anything else, when I heard about the vessel's being assigned to the Coast Guard, I secretly hoped to be the lucky guy. Any shortcomings I may have had as a seaman must have gone largely undetected, since I had reached the rank of Commander. My early commissioned time had been served in destroyers during Prohibition days, carrying out a duty which was unpopular with the American public, but which furnished a young officer with plenty of excitement, thanks to the skill and ingenuity of the rum runners.

There was a wry standing joke among the junior officers of those days that our successes at sea brought us hardship ashore. Six of our destroyers were sent to Key West as a surprise move in 1928. This was a dirty trick on the runners in that area who had been free to operate almost undisturbed for some time. Our degree of success, until they were able to get adjusted to the new situation, ran the price of Cuban rum up in Key West from $6.00 to $14.00 a gallon, in a period of six weeks.

Those were the days when the hastily commissioned destroyers were undermanned, due to a shortage of officers in this suddenly expanding activity. The result was that many junior officers were thrust into positions of responsibility. I served temporarily as executive officer of a destroyer for eighteen months while still an ensign. Of mistakes I made plenty, but cling to the belief that experience consists of a series of mistakes not too often duplicated. The wonder of the thing is that few of us got into serious trouble during those gay, carefree days.

I went through various classes of vessels as watch officer, navigator, executive officer, and finally as commanding officer of the ship I had left before coming to the Academy. A fair share of close shaves in ship handling had come my way. I had seen a reasonable amount of dirty weather, had served in ships working on stranded vessels and towing disabled craft; had a go at International Ice Patrol, and had been to the Bering Sea and the Arctic. Just prior to our entry into World War II I had taken part in dreary, monotonous weather station duty. All this, I hoped, added up to background experience as a sailorman. Chesty in the knowledge that I had been selected as first skipper of the *Eagle,* my efforts at becoming modesty were almost without

4

humility in the excitement of seeing my name in the orders. It took a few days for ugly doubts to arise.

Nary a finger had I lifted in the actual operation of a sailing ship of any kind. The only sail handling commands I knew were tinged with a heavy Danish accent.

When Denmark was overrun by the Nazis in 1940, her handsome little square-rigged training ship *Danmark* was in Jacksonville, Florida, on an annual cruise. There she was stranded and was befriended by the citizens of Jacksonville. The crew was being fed and clothed by public donations. The situation became known to the Commandant of the Coast Guard and he offered to charter the vessel from the Danish minister-in-exile in Washington. His offer was accepted, and the *Danmark* served out the remainder of the war as a training ship for the Coast Guard Academy.

Through the summers of 1943, '44, and '45 I went along on her cruises, which were confined to Long Island Sound and the Martha's Vineyard area. She was still operated by her Danish captain and officers. The Danes were experts. I had been a fascinated watcher as the *Danmark* beat to windward in the confined waters of eastern Long Island Sound. The captain would hold his course on a tack until the bowsprit almost touched the beach before coming about. I had seen him go booming into Great Salt Pond at Block Island under full sail, round to at an anchorage, and have all sails furled in nineteen minutes. Whenever there was a fair breeze, it was his conceit to enter New London harbor under full sail and squeeze through the narrow drawbridge without the use of power. The clearance between ship and bridge abutments was so scanty that the yards had to be braced around to permit this dangerous piece of showmanship. Old timers in the community who recognized the superlative skill involved, would flock to the waterfront to watch this grandstand act when the *Danmark* was sighted inbound.

All this time I had not taken part in the maneuvering of the ship. I had overall responsibility for seamanship instruction and could see no reason for stepping on the Danish skipper's toes when this was his racket. In the course of our batting around the Sound, we went through the exercises of hoisting and lowering boats, riding at a sea painter, and holding endless man-overboard drills. Most of my time was spent in a deck chair on the quarterdeck as an interested observer, while the heads of the various departments carried on with the actual work.

In the summer of 1944 we were treated to a tropical hurricane. At the time I was in my usual status as a cabin guest. When the hurricane struck we were at the western end of Long Island Sound near City Island, New York. The ship rode out the storm to two anchors steaming slow ahead, just south of Stepping Stones Lighthouse, with a broad mud flat to leeward for an easy grounding in case the anchors failed to hold. As the residents of New York and Connecticut can testify, this storm gave the area a good dusting.

Watching the Danes get the ship ready for the storm added to my store of professional knowledge in case I should ever get caught in a harbor with a square-rigger. Every sail on board was either sent below decks or tightly furled with extra lashings. All the loose lines aloft were securely fastened with sail twine at intervals of 12 to 18 inches, to prevent vibration in the wind and resultant wearing.

I took my station in the comfortable cabin alongside a radio, and just let her blow while I followed the progress of the storm as told by excited news announcers. At one point I grew so bold as to crack the cabin door and have a peep outdoors. One peep was enough. The roaring wind and hammering rain made it very uncomfortable for people who had to be out in it. I hurried back to the radio, and kept informed of the ship's safety by way of intermittent conversations with the ship's officers as they occasionally stopped in the cabin for a cigarette or a cup of coffee. This storm behaved in a normal text-book fashion and blew itself out in a few hours. The *Danmark* came through, thanks to the skill of her permanent officers, without a nickel's worth of damage.

In my contact with the *Danmark*, I became very friendly with the executive officer, a man of twenty-five years' experience in square-rigged ships of various kinds. During a sailing maneuver the captain would appear on the quarter-deck with a big megaphone and take his station alongside the helmsman. As he aimed the megaphone forward and bellowed his commands, it seemed to me that the instant obedience to those orders was the result of the word of the next maneuver having been quietly passed along ahead of the command by the soft-spoken, self-effacing executive officer. It made a good show, especially to the uninitiated. The smart, efficient maneuvering of the *Danmark* up and down the Sound brought favorable comment for her and for the Academy from points all over the area, and especially from the many yachtsmen who are dedicated to the principle that the only real yachting is under sail.

My experience on the *Danmark*, although entertaining to a high degree, and instructive in a limited sense, was by no means a complete qualification for a master of a square-rigger. The reasoning that "In a village of blind men, a one-eyed man is king," must have guided the ones who wrote my orders. I was the Coast Guard's one-eyed man.

Modern books on sailing ships aren't very helpful when it comes to actual operation. Few people know anything about running a square-rigger, with the rare exception of Alan Villiers, whose valuable works had not yet come to my attention, and whose very best book, The Way of a Ship, had yet to be written. True, some authors discussed tacking, wearing, box hauling and veering with authority, but never in enough detail for a poor soul who wanted to know everything about halyards and braces, inhauls and outhauls, gaskets and clews, fife rails and pin rails. Maybe something would come to me out of having seen this gear in operation. I cursed every moment spent in idleness on the *Danmark* when I could have been sopping up knowledge and storing it away. It was too late. She had set sail for Denmark a month ago.

The pre-commissioning party consisted of me as Prospective Commanding Officer, two junior line officers and one engineer officer, plus four or five petty officers. The remainder of the crew was to follow at a later date. There was some doubt about how many men would finally be sent. Reserve personnel were adding up points for release from the service. There was nothing glamorous about remaining in, now that the war was over. The second class cadets at the Academy were to be shipped over to fill out the crew, if it was certain that the *Horst Wessel* would arrive in New London before graduation week in June. In the blithe assurance that this arrival date would be met, I put my mind at rest so far as the manpower problem was concerned.

The advance party was to take off from LaGuardia Field. There was an air of tingling excitement as we prepared for the trip. The days of high adventure were not dead! Visions of billowing sails against the blue skies of the northeast trades temporarily allayed the nagging fears and feelings of inadequacy that had been so much a part of every day during the past few weeks.

My crew and I got to Fort Totten, New York, early, having left New London at dawn. Our naive belief was that we would be quickly processed and hauled to LaGuardia where the plane would then take off and fly us to Germany. We hustled over to the passenger processing office, confident that our Class Two priorities would put us

8

at the head of the list. There was a milling mob around the counter. *All* the fifty-odd people in the room had Class Two priorities. A young lieutenant entered and asked to be heard.

"You are to go over to the briefing room."

"What's it all about?"

"All passengers get a pre-flight briefing on flight procedure, ditching exercises, and general information about what's going on on the other side of the world. The first briefing period starts in five minutes. Names and flight numbers will be announced six hours before departure. Please do not leave the area for any purpose, without special permission, after you have been alerted. You will have to wait here on the Post until you are alerted so you will know when your six-hour period starts."

Six hours!

The briefings lasted the whole day, with a short pause for lunch. The first period was devoted to a lecture on the dangers of native foods in tropical lands. We looked at each other in wonderment. The next lecture was about the prevalence of venereal disease in the Middle East. This was all very interesting. That afternoon they scared the daylights out of us with a movie on ditching. We were required to sit in horrified astonishment while a plane just like the one we were going to ride, crashed into the ocean. We were told how many minutes this plane could be expected to float, allowing us time to get into a self-inflating raft. The movie ditching obviously took place in a warm, tropical sea. Our course was over Labrador, over Davis Strait, across the southern tip of Greenland, over Iceland and on to Europe in the middle of January. Perhaps the briefings were designed to subdue the passengers. Nothing we saw or heard inspired overconfidence.

At the end of the day we were called together and told that we could expect to be alerted some time between

9

six P.M. and midnight. We wandered aimlessly around wondering what to do with ourselves. In the Red Cross hut we became involved in a lackadaisical shuffleboard contest. With occasional breaks for coffee, we slid the little steel disks back and forth on the sanded runway until three A.M. No alerts. One by one my party wandered off, looking for a place to sleep.

A droning noise like the swarming of bees led me to the barracks sleeping room. As I opened the door, the impact of the chorus of snores and the fetid air were almost a physical blow. The smell was reminiscent of a gymnasium dressing room. The heat was on full blast. A try at the lights in order to find my bunk brought a growled "Turn off the damned light!" Timidly, I snapped it off and groped around in the darkness until I came to an unoccupied bunk. I didn't care whose it was. I fell across it and dropped into a half dozing stupor. Somehow the night passed.

Next morning we pestered the passenger window attendant until he passed out the information that our flight was postponed for another twelve hours. We were told that the news might change and that we had better stay close to the office for additional announcements. A new officer came on duty and directed us to go to the briefing room. I sneaked out and headed for the Red Cross shack, where I ran into the rest of my gang. We had no stomach for more briefings. The shuffleboard game resumed.

The big news came at noon. Our names were called and we were told to "embus" at five P.M. We would then be hauled to LaGuardia where we would "debus." At five o'clock sharp we headed for the field. It was a clear, cold evening. The air was calm. A somewhat *subdued* tingle of excitement accompanied our arrival at LaGuardia. Here the business of signing in, surrendering copies of orders, the weighing of baggage, and more briefings took another hour.

By now we had become acquainted with the other passengers who were to make the flight as far as London. I fell into conversation with an army colonel. This was old stuff to him.

"You better load up on such things as fresh milk, bacon and eggs and real fruit juice, because this is the last you're gonna have for a long time."

"Aren't they feeding well in Germany?"

"Oh, you'll get plenty to eat, but you're gonna get awfully tired of powdered eggs, dehydrated potatoes and no fresh milk."

Following his lead, I spent the next forty minutes in the lunch room. I had bacon and eggs, sunny side up. His warning gave the meal added zest. Just as we were finishing, the PA system announced our flight.

With the ominous briefings fresh in mind, there was an air of reluctance in our crowd as we went on board. The steward made his speech:

"This is a plush job. We will take off in a few minutes, and in five and a half hours we will land at Goose Bay, Labrador. We will stop there for forty minutes for a hot meal. We will then fly on to Iceland in eight hours. There will be another forty minute stop there. The flight to London will take eight more hours."

It was really a very nice plane, a C-54, but it showed signs of hard usage. Behind each engine the wings were smoke and grease stained. How much maintenance were these planes getting now that demobilization was going on? Maintenance technicians were swarming home from the wars, leaving the planes to practically look out for themselves. I knew that out in the Pacific, under pressure of the constantly reiterated "Bring our boys home *now*," men were being snatched off ships and "magic carpeted" home so fast that getting the ships back with enough competent personnel to run them was a serious problem in the Navy. So it must have been in the Air Force too. I wondered how long it had been since these four engines had been over-hauled or, for that matter, been given a routine maintenance inspection.

After the engines were started, strange beeping noises filled the passenger compartment as we taxied to our place on the runway. Perhaps this was some sort of alarm! Some ship's general alarms had a similar sound. Had I known that this sinister sound was merely an indication that the hydraulic system in the landing gear was functioning properly, I would have been slightly less uneasy. We taxied for miles and miles. The pilot would stop occasionally and gun the engines, then start up and taxi some more. Just as we were bracing ourselves for the takeoff, all four engines stopped. I peered curiously out the window and discovered that we were back at the loading ramp. The steward opened the big door and the loading ladder was wheeled into place. In a bored voice as though he had made this same announcement many times before:

"All right—get out."

There had been a failure on an oil pressure gauge and the flight would be delayed forty-five minutes. We trooped back into the military lounge. Over another order of bacon and eggs, I asked the colonel:

"Does this sort of thing happen often?"

"Yeah. I've been back and forth four or five times now. The planes seem to be living off their fat. They've got tons of spare parts stacked everywhere you go, but the ground mechanics are scarce as hen's teeth. We seem to fly all right once we get into the air because the engines that are gonna quit usually quit on the runway. The big problem seems to be in getting airborne."

We took off to westward and banked over the heart of New York City as we squared away on our course. The carpet of lights which was midtown Manhattan was a breathtaking sight, but the upsurge of warm air from the streets caused the plane to bounce and lurch in a manner which distracted attention from the view. In a few minutes we were passing over New London. The first hour of the flight went by quickly as we eagerly identified Providence, Boston and Gloucester. In spite of the uneasiness which accompanied the beginning of the flight, I dropped off to exhausted slumber. I woke as the plane was letting down at Goose Bay.

Bearing in mind that forty minutes can be very short if there is any delay in being served, we rushed into the hotel dining room and ordered, to a man, bacon and eggs. This was due to the suggestion by the waitress that bacon and eggs could be had with the least amount of delay. When the forty minutes were almost up, a messenger brought word that the takeoff would be delayed due to engine trouble. One hour. Two hours. Three hours. Word came that the delay would be indefinite. We were assigned rooms.

The hotel, much like a rustic lodge similar to those found in ski resorts, rejoiced in the name of "DeGink." It was a surprisingly comfortable place and must have been splendidly insulated. With the temperature at forty degrees below zero outside, we wandered around the pleasantly warm lobby.

I looked in on a rough, tough poker game for a while, but decided it was too rich for my blood when I found out the value of the chips. The players were mainly flyers who had lost sight of the value of money. Some of them had not been home for many months and were attempting to increase their stake for the big fling in about the most unreliable way I know. Others, stationed there, were throwing their money around out of sheer boredom. I fell in with some bridge players, and the time went by pleasantly.

Next morning the temperature outside was still forty below. All day long the ground crew hauled the plane in and out of the hanger. Each time they tried to get all four

13

engines operating, one or more of them died aborning. The passengers grew bored with these alerts and lost faith in our ability to ever get off the ground. Two and a half days later the plane successfully got into the air.

Iceland greeted us with a rain storm. The change in climate did not improve the health of the engines. We spent a night and a day at Reykjavik while they tinkered with the plane. The principal item on the bill of fare at the airport restaurant was bacon and eggs.

From Iceland on, one of the starboard engines coughed and spat like a consumptive. I became obsessed with the idea of getting this flight over and never setting foot in a plane again. No matter how rough the sea, a ship on the surface would be my choice forevermore. We were diverted to Prestwick, Scotland, because all England was socked in with fog. Next day we pulled into London, six days out of LaGuardia.

Bad weather held us in England seven days.

The time finally came when we were to fly on to Bremen. Our detachment, worse for wear, met at Bovington Airport. A battered old C-47 was our vehicle. Miscellaneous boxes and packages were piled helter-skelter inside and lashed down in a haphazard fashion. As a seaman called off the names on the manifest, the passengers crawled into the plane. My name was missing. I grabbed up the manifest and wrote my name in. The dispatcher looked astonished but made no protest.

Sitting on the bucket seat next to mine was an individual in the uniform of a navy commander. He wore an expression you sometimes see on the faces of the more squeamish customers in a fish market. In Bremerhaven we logged in together and the billeting office assigned us to the same apartment. There was an air of restraint and an economy of words as we settled our things and went looking for the officers' mess.

The *Horst Wessel* tied up at Bremerhaven.

Most of the sails are clearly visible in this picture. Starting at the tip of the bowsprit the triangular sails forward of the foremast are the flying jib, outer jib, inner jib, and foretopmast staysail.

The largest square sails on the foremast and mainmast are called courses. On these two masts, in the same order moving aloft come the lower topsails, upper topsails, topgallant sails, and royals. The triangular sails between foremast, mainmast and mizzen are staysails, named after the stays to which they are attached. The mizzenmast carries the upper and lower mizzensails and the mizzen topsail.

After dinner we wound up at the officers' club together. Warming over a drink or two, my companion spoke up:

"I've got a confession to make. When we took off at Bovington, I made up my mind that you were about the sourest looking character I had ever seen. Now you seem like a regular guy. What the hell was ailing you?"

"Well, I can't do much about my looks as an everyday matter, but this was my thirteenth day of so-called air travel from New York. It isn't as though I had any harrowing narrow escapes. I've just lost faith in the air transport people to keep their planes running decently. It took my last ounce of guts to get in that patched-up airplane for what I hope is my last time aloft."

On the verge of returning the compliment, I decided against telling him how he had impressed me at first glance. I don't know what his excuse was, but suspect his state of mind arose out of the fact that he, being a reserve officer and a specialist, had served throughout the war close to home, and had never been separated from his family before. Subsequently we became friends, and ended by being shipmates.

Next morning I got my first look at the *Horst Wessel.*

She lay at a bombed-out shipyard amid the ugly skeletons of shattered buildings and mountainous heaps of rubble, her stately masts canted drunkenly to starboard, as she rested on the bottom of a narrow waterway at low tide. Her gray sides were smeared with stains, the paint on her yards and masts blistered and cracked. Raised metal lettering on each side of the quarterdeck informed the world that this was the *Horst Wessel,* a ship of the dead Nazi navy.

The *Horst Wessel* was built at the Blohm and Voss Shipyard in Hamburg in 1937. She is a three-masted bark, 295 feet over all, displaces 1700 tons, and carries 22,000 square feet of sail, give or take a stays'l or two. She has an auxiliary diesel which can be disengaged from the propeller while under sail by means of a clutch on her main shaft.

A bark is so named because of the arrangement of her masts and yards. A three-masted bark (there can be four masts or even five) has two masts fitted with square yards and the third mast, the aftermost, with fore and aft boom and gaffs, much the same as schooners carry. I marveled at the towering height of the mainm'st, which stood 148 feet above the waterline, and tried to imagine what this bedraggled guttersnipe, with her rust streaks and dirt, would look like with a fresh coat of paint and a new suit of sails. Now she was totally out of commission and her yards were bare.

The German navy operated four such vessels in the 1930's, all bark-rigged. Two were lost at sea during the war, and the *Horst Wessel's* sister ship, *Albert Schlageter*, remained at Bremerhaven unclaimed during the fitting out period of her twin. She also had been awarded to the United States, but no American agency wanted her, and she was eventually transferred to Brazil.

After the *Horst Wessel* was completed she made one summer cruise in the Atlantic. With Hitler making his warlike moves in 1939, she remained in the vicinity of the Baltic Sea. At the outbreak of World War II she was confined entirely to the Baltic, and when the big retreat before the Soviet army was begun, she was pressed into service evacuating women and children southward along the coast. At the very end of the war she narrowly escaped total destruction by failing to arrive at her port of destination on time. She had been directed to proceed to Kiel, and arriving near the harbor entrance after dark, lay offshore until daylight. That fateful night a king-sized air raid hit Kiel. A rain of bombs did frightful damage ashore and sank every vessel in the harbor. Upon seeing the impossibility of carrying out his orders, the captain proceeded independently to Flens-

18

burg, where the vessel remained the few days that were left of the war.

The turning over of the remnants of the German navy to the Allied Forces was a simple and well ordered affair. Upon assurance being given that they would not engage in sabotage, the Germans were allowed to remain in their ships, and assisted in disarming the vessels and disposing of ammunition and other explosives. When we arrived, the *Horst Wessel* was still manned by Germans. We were directed to proceed with the fitting out, using that crew and a nearby German shipyard force as manpower.

Chapter II

Fitting out the *Horst Wessel* was a project of the U. S. Navy, under whose control she was to remain until sailing day, at which time she would pass into Coast Guard jurisdiction. As Prospective Commanding Officer during the fitting out period, I had no authority to give orders, but I could object to work I thought unsatisfactory and could refuse to take the ship out until, in my opinion, it was in all respects ready for sea. From beginning to end I was never in any controversy with the Navy. As soon as I arrived, I discovered that I would have a free hand in the selection of stores and spare parts *if* the things we needed could be found.

Two big shortages existed—material things such as tools, spare parts, sail cloth, ropes and lines of various sizes—and the intangible ingredient: the knowhow necessary to take a square-rigger unescorted across the Atlantic. My crew and I set to work dividing our time between searching out the tangibles and studying the operation of the complex rigging. What happened below decks was important, but secondary.

I was given an office in the Headquarters building of the Commanding Officer, Naval Advance Base, located in a former German naval school—a group of ugly red buildings with steep gabled roofs near the center of Bremerhaven. A narrow muddy stream separated the naval base from the *Horst Wessel's* berth. In order to get from my office to the ship, it was necessary to drive through town to the nearest bridge and back upstream on the far side to the shipyard, a distance of about three miles.

Bremerhaven in 1946.

The *Horst Wessel* seen from a bombed out building.

After my brief and discouraging first look at the *Horst Wessel,* I went into the routine of preliminary visits to the various officers who had a finger in the pie. In order to go about the job of scrounging for parts and material, I sought the advice of some of the old timers about the probable whereabouts of the needed stuff. Regardless of the fact that I was a stranger to the *Horst Wessel's* rig, my training qualified me to know in general terms what was needed.

Getting from office to ship involved an automobile trip, but I could walk from my quarters to the office in a few minutes. Old Sourpuss and I had been quartered in a clammy, dimly lit apartment alongside the imposing stone gate leading into the Base. With lukewarm bath water and insufficient heat, it was perfectly clear that permanent residents would not accept these quarters without a howl. After a couple of days our howling got results from the billeting office, and we were moved out into town where a community of naval officers lived, still within easy walking distance.

Our new apartment was the middle floor of a three-story building. Below lived a Navy dentist in solitary splendor. Above resided two junior officers, who were either cowed by the rank below or were model young men who lived a life of stainless propriety. We never heard them come or go, nor did we hear a sound from overhead, and only knew they were there because each apartment had a 'phone outlet from one incoming line. When the 'phone would ring, whoever answered would bang one, two, or three times on the nearest steam pipe to indicate which floor the call was for.

Our building was at the end of a row of almost identical houses along one city block. Across the street was a boggy marsh that extended a hundred yards or so to a railroad running parallel to the street. The passing trains attracted my attention because of their peculiar European construction and their squealing little whistles. Every evening just before five, a long freight would pass westbound, loaded with hundreds of miserable looking people. These were DP's, bound from Nowhere to Nowhere. Although our street's name was Frulingstrasse, it was popularly known as "Fraulinestrasse," because of the regular appearance of fraulines at the officers' club in the middle of the block.

The new apartment stood, fully furnished, just as the former occupant had lived in it. The two comfortable bedrooms were connected by a large living room. Heavy Germanic furniture, dominated by an enormous grandfather's clock which would have been appropriate in Grand Central Station, made the rooms seem smaller than they really were. The double toned bonging of the hours and half hours rang throughout the building.

The apartment was heated by a coal burning furnace and was cozy and warm. The bay window of the living room was filled by a platform about twelve inches high, on which was a small writing desk and a chair. The three windows of the bay gathered a maximum amount of the pale wintry light of this high latitude. This provided a convenient spot for preparation of my daily progress reports.

As we congratulated ourselves on falling heir to Persian rugs, Dresden figurines and a hodge-podge collection of glassware, some really fine crystal mixed in with gleanings from the North German Lloyd and Hamburg-American Lines, we agreed that we were going to be quite comfortable in these new diggings.

Two days later my apartment mate was transferred to Bremen.

Although by this time I had taken a liking to him, I welcomed my new privacy. It was going to be good to sit down at the end of a day and appraise the ship's work and have a quiet place for the composing of progress reports for the people at home. The following afternoon when I came in

23

from work, I found a new apartment mate, another commander, scratching about and getting himself settled.

A man of average height and stocky build, fiftyish, his closely shaven chin concealed the fact that his whiskers ran to gray. He had the clear blue eyes of a much younger person, the pale shade of blue so common among seafarers. His poker face was non-committal. I was prepared to dislike him for this invasion of my new-found privacy. After we introduced ourselves, I retired to my room while he unpacked his gear. Soon there came a tap on my door.

"It's five o'clock. I call five o'clock gin time. Come out and join me."

Over a mixture of gin and canned orange juice, I learned something of his background. He was born in the Netherlands and had traveled the world. In the International Settlement in Shanghai he had picked up his nickname, "Ducky," which is roughly a translation of his surname. His civilian business had something to do with insurance, but his main interest in life was yachting, principally ocean racing. Since the Coast Guard has always been involved in yacht racing, my contacts and knowledge of some of the facets of this sport gave us a common meeting ground. As we talked, his infrequent smile revealed a pair of almost girlish dimples.

When you have spent some years living in wardrooms, you become accustomed to the keen sizing up job which goes on when a new member joins the mess. The newcomer must take with good grace the searching examination which goes on as the oldsters try to ascertain the "cut of his jib." Ducky and I were giving each other the once-over.

After a period of polite exchanges, Ducky asked a question that was put to me almost every day:

"What is the Coast Guard doing in Germany?"

"We've come over to get the *Horst Wessel.*"

"You a sailor?"

"I don't know how to answer that question. According to the standards of a veteran of Bermuda races, the answer is perhaps 'No.' I've done a little, and have been exposed to square-riggers to the extent of riding around on the *Danmark* when she was at New London. If we meet in the States after this adventure is over, ask that question again."

Ducky's manner instantly changed. All the starch went out of his speech.

"That's a terrific assignment. Wish I could join you. We could have a hell of a time."

"Why don't you? I could use the help of an honest-to-goodness sail man."

"I'd like nothing better, but I've just got this new assignment."

Ducky was the new assistant to the Chief-of-Staff, aiding him in his mission of disposing of the remainder of the German fleet assigned to the United States forces. He had been transferred from Berlin, where he had served on a sub-board having to do with the division of the ships of the German navy, so he knew all about the *Horst Wessel*. He had a photographic memory. During the short period since the German surrender he had acquired an enormous store of knowledge of the German fleet, extending into the most minute details of individual ships. Our casual conversation that first afternoon provided clues to the whereabouts of some of the much needed material for my ship. Even ashore, Ducky was going to be a great help to me.

Every working day at noon all of the officers ate at the commissioned officers' mess at the Naval Base. We were placed strictly according to rank; that is, the naval officers were. Somehow the billeting officer overlooked asking my date of rank. The assumption was that I was very, very junior, probably because my blues had shiny new stripes on them, a last minute renewal just before leaving the States.

Eating among the very junior officers made for lively conversation.

At the entrance way to the mess hall there was a row of cubby holes for personal napkins. They were marshaled in military order, with the chief-of-staff's at the far left nearest the door. Napkin rings were rubber bands from the office, and identification was achieved by penciling initials on the corner of the napkins. Mine reposed in the last cubby hole of commanders' row.

The Chief-of-Staff, a very senior captain with strict standards of protocol, as evidenced by the mathematical gradation in napkin stowage, fell in alongside me as we were going to lunch one day. I nipped over to his left and fell into step.

"That's quite a sporting job you have, Mac. Wish I could go along."

"I've got fingers crossed on both hands, Captain, hoping we'll find enough stuff for a proper fitting out and praying for good weather on the way home."

"Oh, you'll make out all right. By the way, how long have you been in the Coast Guard?"

"I was commissioned in '26, Captain."

"You were! What is your date of rank?"

"October, '42."

"Good gosh, you don't look that old."

He moved on ahead of me, and flagged the executive officer. I pretended not to notice that the exec was getting a whispered "chewing out" about something.

After lunch, I absent-mindedly rolled my napkin and snapped on the rubber band. I reached toward the customary cubby hole, only to find that my name had been erased and a strange napkin was where mine ordinarily lived. As I ticked off the spaces up the line, I finally came to the spot which revealed that my napkin had been promoted from the tailend Charley position to the space just

26

above the executive officer and next below the junior captain. My napkin had leap-frogged the entire lot of commanders—a fast promotion.

Each night after gin time Ducky and I would set out in one of the vehicles which were assigned to us, to eat at the place of our choice. Occasionally we went to the officers' mess at the naval station in Bremerhaven, but we were at liberty to visit the senior naval officers' mess out in town, or we could drive over to Bremen and dine in style at the very swank officers' club. The "swank" was achieved through the addition of German orchestras and the acquisition of a few selected wines. The basic ration was unvaried. The colonel at LaGuardia had been right. We had frequent servings of powdered eggs, dehydrated potatoes and pressed ham. Sometimes a mess would employ an exceptional German chef who could manage to eke out mediocre miracles, but the plain fact was the food was monotonous, and we ate with lack-lustre appetites.

This sharpened our acquisitive sense and we became expert scroungers. We kept on good terms with our downstairs neighbor, who was "keeping company" with an attractive frauline. It was their custom to go out into the country on Saturday afternoons and in the course of the trip, trade with the farmers: cigarettes for eggs.

Cigarettes were rigidly rationed by the armed forces, the limit being one carton a person a week. At the same time American magazines printed for overseas distribution carried advertisements running something like this: "Your favorite brand of cigarette delivered anywhere in the world absolutely tax free, 60¢ a carton, available in lots of five and ten cartons." The military postal authorities, so far as I could tell, never intercepted any of these shipments, which were arriving regularly addressed to armed forces personnel who wanted some of the niceties which were otherwise forbidden by regulation. Although we did not do the trading, we were regular recipients of some of these niceties.

We hoarded eggs for Sunday brunch at home. We swiped bread from the officers' mess. Our bacon came from a special category of ten-in-one army field rations. These rations were not being issued to the troops and were supposedly locked up in quartermaster warehouses. Nevertheless, some of the bacon was always in circulation. Ours came from someone who got it from someone who got it from someone. By constant searching and scrounging we managed to have our Sunday brunches well supplied.

Ducky's native Dutch enabled him to communicate effectively with Anna, the German hausfrau who was assigned to keep our quarters clean. She spoke no English and conveyed her wants for soap, starch and mending materials by way of Ducky's Teutonic ear. His arrival must have been as welcome to Anna as it was helpful to me.

The day before he showed up, as I was leaving for work, Anna stopped me at the front door and asked me a question in German. I could only look puzzled and shrug my lack of comprehension. She raised her voice slightly and enunciated with great care, repeating the question. I gave her another blank look. Soon Anna was shouting her question at the top of her voice, which, I suppose, she hoped would break down my wall of ignorance by sheer force. The disturbed downstairs neighbor, an old occupation hand, came to the rescue and explained that Anna wanted soap, starch and shoe polish to properly carry out her duties. That afternoon I made a point of picking up a handbook of simple spoken German, but I was excused from any more shouting sessions by Ducky's timely arrival.

Anna had the ageless face of the burgher hausfrau. We guessed her to be about fifty-five. In short order, Ducky, Anna and I were adjusted. Anna would appear in the mornings just as we were leaving for work. In the afternoon as we came in from our separate ways, she would go bouncing down the stairs with a cheery "Auf weidersehen!" The apartment would be sparkling. Her last act of the day would have been to scrub the stairs leading to the landing below, so that we would find them just dry as we came in. The underwear, shirts and socks negligently tossed aside by her two careless masters would be washed, pressed, mended and neatly stowed in the wardrobes, the spare shoes shined and placed in the little cabinets alongside the beds. In gratitude for this service, we handed over our weekly candy ration for Anna's daughter and her daughter's children. The sacrifice was small, since neither Ducky nor I cared for candy.

One Friday afternoon, in an expansive mood, we decided to give Anna a special reward. From a freshly opened can of our precious bacon we invited her to help herself. Sunday morning we discovered that she had taken us literally. The whole two-pound can was gone! At the time it seemed terribly important. Luxury foods had no fixed market price. They ranked somewhere along with religion.

Things were never dull around Ducky. New facets of his complex personality cropped up every day. He played a masterful game of bridge. He was an extremely rugged and skillful sailorman, as attested by the ocean racing fraternity. I thought his chilly hostility to Germans in general revealed a cold streak in his personality, until I discovered that his feeling of animosity was pointed and personal. His brother and sister, accused of spying, had been thrown in jail by the Gestapo just before the end of the war. The story goes that Ducky, in his jeep, was following a column of tanks as the troops were advancing through Holland. He grew impatient with the slow progress, found a parallel side road, and roared on ahead of the advancing troops to liberate his home town singlehanded.

Ducky's attitude toward M.P.'s was, to say the least,

remarkable. There were two gates leading from the marine school headquarters into the town. One was reserved for Navy personnel and the other for the Army. The Army gate was closest to the senior officers' mess; so Ducky used that gate. Each time the M.P.'s stopped him and explained the segregation of the gates, they received an icy stare and a stern reminder that they should confine their activities to soldiers and not bother innocent naval officers. He contemptuously destroyed a long series of traffic tickets. None of the rest of us would have dreamed of doing the things Ducky did. We all waited for him to get his comeuppance, but he lived a charmed life.

The story went the rounds (neither confirmed nor denied by him) that he had been transferred from Berlin for sassing an admiral. I am sure he was capable of this without batting an eye if he thought the admiral was wrong and he was right. He made frequent trips to The Hague with no authorization whatsoever. He would drive up to the frontier and bluff his way past the British guards. In flawless Dutch he managed to convey the impression to the Netherlanders that he was on a secret mission of high priority. His only business was to visit his family. Secretly, he was as sentimental as an Irishman, but had a mortal fear of anyone's finding it out.

One evening I returned to the apartment to find Ducky entertaining guests—*German* guests. Furthermore, he had unbent to the extent of becoming downright jovial in the presence of the hated Hun. He introduced his principal guest, who had been one of the contestants in the 1938 Bermuda Race, and who was well known in American yachting circles. As captain of one of Germany's sea raiders during the war, he had to his credit the sinking of a British cruiser, but in Ducky's books, an honest ocean racing yachtsman could do no wrong.

The matter of transportation was a major problem for

30

everyone, Americans and Germans alike. After the surrender the Allied forces took over all German automobiles and placed them in motor pools in the service of the occupation forces. Since no non-military vehicles had been manufactured in Germany for over six years, transportation for the civilians was grim. When I heard that I would be issued a sedan for use on official business, I felt quite set up. Then I got a look at my prize.

It was a tiny thing with a front wheel drive, a Trumpf-Adler. It was dirty gray in color, and the greasy worn upholstery, with broken springs here and there, testified to hard usage and indifferent maintenance. In the beginning the quiet little engine, about the size of a bread box, ran like a watch. As assorted ailments developed, ranging from minor ignition trouble to complete collapse, I made regular visits to the motor pool. I was repaid for my loving care by a series of unreasoning malfunctions and mechanical trauma. I went through the late senile stages to final interment of the little Adler, to a super-luxurious Mercedes Benz, which gave up the ghost in the outskirts of Bremerhaven with burned out main bearings.

Ducky had an Opel. It ticked right along the whole time he was in Germany, this in spite of his extreme indifference to the welfare of the little beast.

As an economy measure, the use of good American military vehicles was denied to us as long as the occupation people had German stuff to draw on. Left to the German in the street was a choice between walking and fighting his way on board the ancient trolley cars which somehow had been put back in commission after the bomb damage. Allied forces were forbidden to ride the street cars because of their already saturated condition. They were packed with people from early dawn till the curfew hour in the evening.

There were not enough German automobiles to meet the

needs of the Americans who had to move about in the conduct of their business and the motor pools were augmented with old battle damaged, worn out jeeps. It was possible to draw a jeep for a short trip from time to time, and for this purpose the motor pool employed German drivers. After one hair-raising trip of this sort with a wild-eyed German youth, who drove as though he were imbued with the death urge, I went back to the insignificant inconvenience of driving for myself.

To be issued a sedan was, in general, a recognition of rank. Commanders and captains drew sedans. Lieutenant-commanders and down bounced along in jeeps. These jeeps were a special breed of car. Experience with the undulating brick paved side roads of Germany had taught that vehicles with normal springs and a short wheel base, when traveling over thirty miles an hour, were liable to leap off the road whenever they crossed one of the many invisible dips brought about by years of wear. To prevent this the jeep springs were strapped down, making the vehicle as rigid and rough as a farm wagon. The rider, rather than the springs, took the shocks of the rough roads. There was a special technique to riding these automotive abominations. It consisted of leaning slightly forward and absorbing the shocks through the hinge-like arrangement between the backbone and the pelvis. Some beginners developed "jeepitis," which was either a mild back injury or kidney damage.

As bad as they were, there were not enough jeeps to go around. Result: wholesale "borrowings." The motor pool would issue a piece of chain and a padlock with which to lock the steering wheel in a manner designed to make the vehicle unsteerable by the thief. Failure to remember to use this locking device made it absolutely certain that the jeep would be gone almost as soon as it was vacated by the driver. My exec had his jeep stolen five times. Each time it was recovered the following day abandoned somewhere nearby.

The need for transportation arose from the fact that a military installation was never a compact unit, but was scattered about throughout the area, making use of housing and office space which had withstood war damage. This required some miles to be covered in the ordinary business of a day's work—from sleeping place to eating place to working place, and back again.

An early move of the Occupation had been to place some of the German breweries in commission, and we were able to get excellent beer for five cents a glass. That's a drink of which I am especially fond, and sometimes I would sit around until the club closed, enjoying good beer and good talk.

One midnight as I was leaving the club through the door in the high walled garden, my hat was snatched from my head and went sailing off into the darkness. A storm had swept in off the North Sea, but in the sheltered confines of the club it had not been noticed. A commander's hat, with the scrambled eggs on the visor, is expensive. That was bad enough, but even worse, I was the only Coast Guard Commander in all of Europe, and it might take weeks to replace this, my only hat. An officer of the sea forces is never caught outdoors bareheaded. I might as well be dead if I could not find it.

Once, as a junior watch officer, I saw a grizzled old commander poke his head incautiously out a bridge window. Away went his shiny new topper overboard. His violent reaction had shocked me. He leaped to the general alarm and sounded "man overboard." The drill went off smoothly and the boat was away in good time. It got within ten feet of the hat, but the headgear sank from sight before the bow-hook could grab it. The old guy's ranting and swearing seemed unreasonable and out of proportion. Now I could appreciate his feelings.

Cars coming toward me on the one-way street lit up the road but failed to point out the priceless headgear. I went from house to house looking in front yards, crossing and re-crossing the street, peering into ditches. It was cold and rainy. The hat had to be found in a hurry or it would be ruined. My frantic search extended to the end of the street. No hat. Aside from the fact that I would be a laughing stock, a silly accident was going to seriously affect my usefulness.

When I got back to the apartment, Ducky had already turned in, and I had no one to tell my troubles to. I slumped into a chair in the living room without bothering to take off my overcoat. This utterly ridiculous accident was brought about by the fact that I had traveled by air and the baggage permitted was limited. An officer's uniform cap is a cumbersome thing to pack. The confounded thing just will not fit anywhere decently in baggage. Naval officers' caps were around me in plenty. If only I had had brains enough to bring a cap device in my pocket, I would not be in trouble now. Judging by the slowness of air mail in this bad weather, it might take weeks to get a new one from the States.

With this bleak outlook I turned in. Thank goodness for the nickel beer at the club. In spite of my predicament, I managed to get a night's dreamless sleep.

Next morning, a Sunday, I leaped out of bed at sunrise, dressed hurriedly, and rushed out to resume the search. There was a detachment of soldiers billeted at the downwind end of the street. I went into the day room and offered a ten dollar reward for the finder of my hat. Soldiers spewed out of the building like bees from a hive. This was between paydays. They covered every inch of the ground for half a mile. By mid-morning there were a lot of dis-

34

appointed soldiers, and my last glimmer of hope had died.

I mounted the steps of the apartment through a cloud of black despair, tottered across the living room and collapsed into a chair. My eyes wandered incuriously to the living room table. In the center there was a mirage. It looked for all the world like a Coast Guard Commander's hat. Cautiously I sneaked up on the illusion. It was real. It *was* my hat! It was clean but damp. I burst into Ducky's room and shook him awake.

"Ducky, my hat! How did it get there?"

"Are you crazy? Get out of here and let me get some sleep."

I persisted: "How did my hat get back here in the apartment?"

"I don't know anything about your damn hat. Now clear out of here."

When Ducky came out of his room, grumpy over his rude awakening, I told him what had happened the night before. His look of disbelief was all the proof needed that the hat incident had better be suppressed. No one was going to believe that the darn thing had flown against the wind and landed in my own living room.

I was free of the agony of embarrassment over the loss of the hat, but the miracle of its reappearance hinted of witchcraft. In the midst of my baffled speculation, the 'phone rang. It was the downstairs neighbor.

"Did you find your hat all right?"

"Yes, but how it got in my living room . . ."

"That's easy. *I* put it there. I found it in the middle of the street opposite our front door early this morning. It had some mud on it and I washed it off. Hope it's all right. A look at the device told me who the owner was."

"Thanks a million, old man. You've saved my life. The thing that gets me is that I lost that hat about five hundred yards downwind in a sixty-mile breeze last night. How the thing could sail upwind, I'll never know."

We discussed all the possibilities, and decided that it must have landed on the radiator of a car and bounced off after it was brought this far. I hoped my guardian angel was just warming up. If this was a sample of performance, prospects for the trip home were rosy indeed.

Chapter III

The first day I went on board the *Horst Wessel* I was received with full military honors, the young German skipper smiling politely as he stood stiffly at hand salute. This was repeated upon departure. The same thing happened the next day, and the next.

I was flattered and a little embarrassed by this fanfare. Their eagerness to do the correct military thing dispelled a lot of the uneasiness in approaching my former enemies I had felt on the way over; but, in fact, the German Navy no longer existed, and the rendering of these honors seemed a little silly.

The first time a German sailor passed me on deck, he snapped to a rigid brace as he walked by, and followed me with his eyes until his neck was craned over his shoulder, as though his head were on a swivel. I bristled with suspicion, thinking he was staring at me contemptuously. Upon meeting a man in a passageway, I got another example of German military behavior. He flung his body flat against the bulkhead, standing stiffly, with his chin pointing almost to the overhead, and remained in this position while I passed.

It took me several days to get used to the rigid rules of conduct so scrupulously observed by these people. The crew members, when on duty, quick-marched about the ship in a parade ground manner. There was nothing of the relaxed atmosphere of American shipboard life. At the same time, they appeared to be cheerful and there were no signs of discontent. The general bearing of the crew made it clear that morale was high. This struck me as strange.

37

Never having seen the aftermath of a war, I had not until now given a thought to how defeated men behaved. Of one thing I was sure—my great granddaddy in Mississippi could not have had this attitude when he came in contact with Yankees after 1865, if my grandmother's yarns were to be believed.

The first time I entered one of the compartments the bellowed "Achtung!" of a petty officer seemed to jerk the men off the benches. This brought memories of spy stories where German agents were supposedly betrayed by leaping to attention when an Allied interrogating officer unexpectedly barked "Achtung!"

After a third day of full honors, shrilling pipes and clicking heels, I had had enough. The former skipper was persuaded that the spit-and-polish could be done away with and that the crew should devote their attention to the business of getting the ship ready for sea.

Before our contingent left the States, the *Horst Wessel* had been visited by the Coast Guard representative from London, for a quick appraisal of the work necessary to prepare her for sea. During that visit of inspection the language barrier introduced errors into the calculations of the fitting out time.

The *Horst Wessel's* captain, while speaking English, occasionally thought in German, and sometimes mistook questions for statements of fact. He was asked the question: "The sails are in good condition, aren't they?" Rather than disagree with his visitor's statement, he had answered in the affirmative. Actually, the best sails on the ship had had hard usage and needed replacement. He had given the same kind of answer when asked about the condition of the main engine.

I examined the machinery records and found that the main engine had not been opened for inspection for over six thousand hours of operation. And so it went. Before leav-

38

ing New London, I had been handed a copy of an optimistic preliminary report on the ship's condition. It turned out to be practically worthless.

The German captain was thirty-five years of age. He bore the rank of Kapitain-Leutnent. He loved his ship and his crew. When he discussed problems with his officers or directed the crew members, he bore the stamp of leadership, without harshness. At all times he upheld the dignity of his subordinates.

As a mark of affection, German enlisted men use a diminutive when addressing an officer. When the captain gave an order, the acknowledgment was always: "Ja-wohl, Herr Ka-Leut."

"Herr Ka-Leut" was tall and thin. He had a musical baritone voice of remarkable range and color. He was blond and handsome in a hawklike way. His acquiline features gave him a distinguished appearance. Add a monacle and the type casting would be perfect. His English pronunciation was excellent, but his thinking in German brought about numerous misunderstandings. However, a few weeks of daily association, in which the Americans were gaining an inkling of German, while the Germans continued to polish their English, brought about a degree of harmony, and the misunderstandings became rare.

Daily association with Herr Ka-Leut brought about a gradual change in our relationship. He never varied from his meticulous politeness, but a warmth bordering upon firm friendship crept into the atmosphere. Little by little, I began to see World War II and its effects through his eyes.

We fell into a daily routine that began with coffee together in the cabin. Although the sideboys and piping had been abolished, Ka-Leut still met me at the gangway and we would go aft together. I would open with, "Guten morgen, Herr Ka-Leut."

He would reply, "Good morning, Cap-tain."

Ka-Leut (left) and The Skipper.

Here the bi-lingual exchange would end. Although I got hold of a phonograph recording course in spoken German and practiced alone at night, my progress was too slow to help with the business on board ship.

"How have things gone since last night?"

The answer would always be the same, "Excellent, Captain," although there were times when we both knew this was not so. The difficulties and emergencies which had arisen during my absence would gradually be uncovered. His was a difficult role. Just where he stood in connection with authority for the job of overhaul was never made quite clear. Under the circumstances, he did remarkably well. Unlike the accepted idea of German military behavior, he showed a lot of initiative by going ahead and getting jobs done without constantly referring to the U.S. Navy for directives.

One morning as we were finishing our coffee, Ka-Leut beamed at me and said:

"I am so glad now that the ship has the order."

He caught my puzzled look.

"That we are going to sail together to America."

I was taken aback. It was news to me that Ka-Leut and his boys were going to be our shipmates. This would come as a jolt to the people at home. They were certain to object when they got word that Germans were coming with us.

Shortly before our trip to Germany, the cruiser *Prinz Eugen* had been delivered to the United States by a German crew, with a few Americans in charge. An incident had taken place in Philadelphia which resulted in unfavorable publicity. American relatives of some of the *Prinz Eugen's* crew had been allowed to go on board bringing food, and joyous reunions had developed into a gay party. This had been picked up by the press and headlined as a scandalous event. Apparently, Ka-Leut had not heard about this. He and his crew were elated over the prospect of making their first visit to the States. Being unsure of how things would finally work out, I turned the conversation to another subject.

I thought it would be foolish at this time to slam the door on the possibility of their making the trip to the States. It was a little cowardly to duck the issue in this fashion, but I suspected that their willing work aboard ship was based on the prospect of making the cruise.

On one occasion Ka-Leut described the last days of the war on the *Horst Wessel*. Remembering Scapa Flow at the end of World War I, I wanted to know why there had been no published instances of sabotage in the German Navy at the time of the surrender and during the hectic days immediately thereafter. Ka-Leut said that most of the regular German Navy considered themselves professional fighting men and had none of the fanaticism of the Nazi party that, he admitted, did exist among the storm troopers and various other German groups. The behavior of the disciplined element of his Navy, he thought, was strongly influenced by the fact that Grand Admiral Doenitz was in command and the Admiral's last dispatch directed all Germans to capitulate in a legal and orderly fashion. Had the order come from any other source, especially from Hitler's headquarters, the outcome might have been quite different, but Admiral Doenitz was a career Navy man.

He pointed out the spot where the demolition charge had been built into the ship, and explained that under Hitler, all German navy vessels had been ordered destroyed if faced with possibility of capture. Admiral Doenitz had countermanded the order. Upon receipt of his message, Ka-Leut had gathered about him those of his crew known to have stable personalities and unquestioned loyalty, and directed them to stand guard while he personally rendered the demolition charge harmless.

One morning about a month after my arrival, when I

came on board, Ka-Leut's customary smile was missing. He was stiff and formally correct. As we walked aft together, I turned things over in my mind, trying to uncover some thoughtless act on my part which may have brought about this abrupt change. When we got into the cabin, instead of sitting down, he stood by the desk and announced in a colorless voice that he had received word of his mother's death in Bremen, and formally requested permission to go to her funeral. I asked if I could help in any way, but he rather curtly assured me he did not need assistance, and off he went.

Next morning he was back on board. Much of the coolness in his manner had disappeared, but he was subdued and uncommunicative until we had finished our coffee. Without preliminaries, he unwrapped a package. Discarding the paper, he handed me a slender crystal decanter. With a slight smile he said:

"Take this home to your wife. No one I care for is now alive."

Late in the war his only brother was captured in East Germany. His father had died some years before. His wife had deserted him before Germany fell, and had disappeared into East Germany. He had heard that she was a popular figure in the Soviet Officers' clubs.

While he was at his mother's funeral, the burgomeister had seized her apartment. A new family would move in the following day. He was told he would not be allowed to remove any belongings. His parting gesture of defiance was to smuggle out the decanter.

Bremen showed no signs of recovery from the thousand-ton nightly raids. The ruthless seizure of Ka-Leut's home and belongings was understandable to anyone who had made a tour of the ruins the length and breadth of the city. There were thousands of homeless people ekeing out a ratlike existence in bombed out cellars, sleeping under piles of rubbish. A trip to Bremen, Hamburg, or any other large German city, was a stunning experience. Ka-Leut had become "adjusted." The blackened bones of gutted buildings, the awful vistas of miles of untenanted streets, appeared to leave him unmoved.

After he returned from his mother's funeral, Ka-Leut's manner took on an increasing gentleness, suggesting a faint overlay of shock. He smiled often but seldom laughed.

One morning he was red-nosed and sniffling. As we reached the warmth of the cabin, he sneezed explosively.

"Gezundheit!"

"Why do you say that, Cap-tain?" He seemed surprised.

I explained that it was an American custom, but I thought it was of German origin.

"Yes, I know the word, but I never heard it used like that before."

All my life I had heard that the blessing of a sneeze was an old German habit. Now I was beginning to realize that many of my preconceived notions about Germany and the Germans were going to have to be discarded.

My first task was to inspect this ship as I had never inspected a ship before. Once we put to sea I would be utterly committed to reliance on a seaworthiness which *I* had to establish. Equally as important, I had to learn how to run this ship, and part of the business of learning was to begin solving the mystery of the working of these miles of lines.

I had never even seen a bark rig before. (The *Danmark* is a full rigged ship.) My first close look at the complicated maze filled me with despair. As I stood on deck and looked aloft, a full realization of the big job ahead dawned. In the good old days, three years before the mast was what it took to make a deckhand. ("Before the mast" refers to the fo'cas'le. Traditionally, the officers live back aft.)

Postponing the hopeless part of my job, I started my

44

inspection on more familiar ground, and went below decks for an inch by inch look from bow to stern. With Ka-Leut as guide, I crept carefully down a well worn ladder to the first fo'cas'le compartment. As my gold embroidered cap visor poked into the compartment door, I was greeted by my first "Achtung!" The men leaped to the position of attention so violently that I could imagine the faint after-sound of twanging uncoiled steel springs. Ka-Leut appeared surprised when I asked that the men continue their work in our presence, and with an air of reluctance, almost apologetic, passed the word.

The compartment smelled of stale saurkraut. The whole ship had a Germanic smell. This compartment was rectangular and barren. The bulkheads and overhead which had originally been white were now a dingy yellow. The paint was cracked and blistered with age. Bare wood and metal showed through everywhere.

The plain wooden deck of broad teak planks was worn away in busy areas, much like the stair treads often seen in old New England homes. German sailors wear wooden-soled sea boots, and the constant clumping back and forth had taken its toll throughout the ship. These decks were still serviceable, but were certainly going to need renewal before too many years went by. This is an expensive job. Wooden deck planks are scarce on modern American ships, and the men who work at paying seams and calking decks are fewer each year. Thank goodness these decks had been of generous thickness when the ship was built; otherwise they would now be completely worn through.

Aside from various storerooms, the interior space of the ship was principally divided between living spaces and the small engine room. In the engine room there was an M.A.N. diesel engine for propulsion in and out of harbors and for limited use when the ship was becalmed. The other machinery consisted of two diesel generators, two air compressors, a miniature evaporator and condenser operated by a little donkey boiler, and assorted pumps for various purposes.

The seamen's and cadets' quarters were starkly bare. As we moved through the petty officers' quarters of the various grades, and further aft to the officers' living spaces, we went through an ascending scale of grandeur. The ship was so complex that I did not attempt to completely orient myself, compartment by compartment. I was searching for things which must be done before we set sail. I found plenty.

Aside from the worn places in the decks, the hull was in excellent condition. The bright sealing faces, slightly greasy to the touch, on the watertight doors, were a tribute to Ka-Leut's thoroughness. It was obvious that soap and paint were scarce, but I had to concede that his crew had tried their best to keep the ship clean.

Below the living spaces we came to the numerous storerooms and tanks. As I had already guessed by now, most of the storerooms were empty. As we went from compartment to compartment, Ka-Leut translated the various name plate legends for my benefit. The bosun's locker contained pitiful remnants, testifying to the shortness of replacement lines and deck stores toward the end of the war. The welcome aroma of oakum and pine tar was in the air, but the lockers and bins were empty. A few old coils of line, a couple of dull, badly worn marlinspikes, fragments of beeswax, and a rawhide mallet worn down to the metal retaining ring, were all that I could see. The same signs of poverty were painfully evident in the sail locker. The sails were there, as Ka-Leut had said, but they were old and worn and bore many patches.

Halfway through the inspection I was so discouraged I wanted to quit.

"Let's knock off and go get a cup of coffee."

46

"Don't you want to see the rest of the ship, Cap-tain?"

"Oh, yes, but I am seeing too much at one time. We'll come back after I get a notebook, and we'll check every department, step by step."

"Yes, sir. It is a good plan."

In the cabin we talked over the ship's condition and what needed to be done.

"We have had no new sail cloth for over a year, Captain."

"Yes, I can see. On a ship like this it would seem to me that a sailmaker would have enough work to keep him busy all of every day."

"He has been busy, but only in repairing old sails. After the bombing started we could get no cloth, no sail twine, no needles, no grommets, no anything; but," he brightened, "I think maybe many of the things we need were hidden underground. We will be detectives and solve this case together."

I hoped we could justify his optimism.

"Ka-Leut, I have heard that this is an all hand-powered ship."

His eyes lit up as he answered:

"That is right. Young German sailors get much work to do with their muscles on this ship and her sister, the *Schlageter*. They are identical except for a few stays'ls. We steer by hand, we set all sails by hand and we get up the anchor by hand."

This I had to see. My memory went back to pictures portraying the good old days when tough looking sailors in stocking caps and pigtails, labored at the capstan bars to the rollicking rhythm of the old sea chanties. It seemed hardly possible that the Germans would reach so far back in time for the sake of authenticity.

We went to the fo'cas'le and there it was—an enormous hourglass-shaped capstan, right out of the past. Radiating out along the surface of the deck, like spokes in a wheel, were the cleats upon which the sailors maintained their footing while they labored 'round and 'round this torture machine. The shaft led down through the deck to a gear box where the gear ratio delivered enough power to heave in a five thousand pound old-fashioned anchor at a snail's pace. I resolved to compromise with tradition as soon as possible, and find a power windlass for this job. There would be plenty to do in the rigging, without the added benefit of this healthful exercise.

The *Eagle* has no bridge in the conventional sense. The word has come down from the days when there was an actual bridge, somewhat like an elevated catwalk, running across the vessel. It was raised sufficiently for a conning officer to be able to see ahead, as well as to observe the working of the ship's rigging. It was born of necessity when the days of sail overlapped the age of steam, in which ocean-going vessels were using both means for propulsion. The conning officer ranges about the quarterdeck. He directs the men at the wheel, the operation of the sails, and must keep an ear cocked for calls from the lookouts, and an eye constantly aloft when the vessel is under sail.

We went aft to the steering station. The rig consists of three wheels on a single horizontal shaft. When a wheel is turned, the shaft, through a knuckle gear, delivers power to a vertical shaft which, in turn, operates the rudder. The wheels are about six feet in diameter, and extend down through slots in a grating platform, where the helmsmen stand. I grabbed one of the spokes and gave it a pull. It didn't budge. I got up on the platform and grasping a spoke in both hands, heaved with all my strength.

"Is this thing locked?"

"No, Cap-tain, it is very stiff. It takes three men to move. You see, we had a leetle bomb damage—a near miss. I think the rudder is bent. Steering is now very difficult."

48

A recent picture looking aft from the quarter deck.

A recent picture looking forward from the quarter deck.

He was a prophet of the obvious. Here was a big item for the repair list.

The wheel stood out in the open immediately in front of a small deckhouse on the poop deck. Inside there were none of the gauges and indicators which are to be found on a conventional ship's bridge. Along the after bulkhead a chart desk with a plain wooden top was fastened to the deck. On the forward bulkhead was the register from an electric anemometer which was mounted on top of the mainm'st. On the opposite bulkhead above the chart desk, a brass aneroid barometer, nested in a carved teak cradle, was suspended from a hook. Knowing there was a gyro installation on board, I had expected to find a repeater in here out of the weather. This would have made it possible for the officer of the deck, while sneaking a smoke in shelter, to follow the steersmen's conduct. But no. He must take his full watch out in the open with the rest of his gang.

The poop deck, also referred to as the quarterdeck, was broad and spacious, occupying fully one third of the deck area. The deckhouse, containing the chart compartment, also housed a little radio room and the captain's sea cabin, which was just large enough to accommodate the built-in bunk along one side, running fore and aft, and a short leather-upholstered transom at the far end. Once we put to sea, most of my time would be spent here.

The regular cabin, which was reached by going down either of a pair of twin ladders to the welldeck and then proceeding aft along a passageway and through two doors, was much too far from the center of things. Many things can happen while a messenger is en route from OD (Officer of the Deck) to Captain. Often he carries information designed to bring a skipper up all standing, instinctively dashing for the bridge before he is fully awake. From the sea cabin I could be aroused instantly by a shout from the OD.

I tested the mattress. It was hard as a rock, exactly like

51

those cruel Danish mattresses I had tried to sleep on in the *Danmark*. I made a mental note: "Scrounge for a mattress."

Ka-Leut obtained an armful of blueprints and laid them out on the cabin table. Blueprint is a misnomer. The Germans use an entirely different method of producing ship's plans. They were beautifully executed. Each sheet of firm white paper achieved an almost third dimensional quality through the ingenius device of using multicolored lines and shaded areas. I needed no knowledge of German to understand the prints superficially, but saw that there was an enormous job ahead in getting the stacks and stacks of valuable sources of information translated into English.

Many German terms so closely resemble English that they are easily recognizable. Two tank areas below the berth decks were labeled respectively "Trinkwasser" and "Washwasser." This was easy, but I could not figure out why a ship would be fitted with a large tank of fresh water unfit for drinking. Ka-Leut explained that the waste water from the bubbling fountains and from the showers and various other places was drained into the "washwasser" tanks, where it was then reused for scrubbing clothes and removing salt rime from paintwork. This seemed to me to be a good way to foul up a tank to such an extent that it would finally become a disgusting mess. Why not clean all tanks thoroughly and fill them *all* with sweet fresh water? I got no answer from Ka-Leut on that question. They just had never done it that way. Another entry for the notebook.

It was not going to be too difficult to get acquainted with the passageways, the access hatches, the companion ladders and such, but the brass nameplates marking pipelines and electric switches and telephone circuits must all be changed. It would take too long to make all these changes before we left, so I decided to start a checkoff list which would contain only the changes that we *must* have in order to get the ship home. I would let the Academy worry about the fancy work.

My engineer officer tapped at the door.

"Cap'n, we've got a hell of a job down below."

"I'm beginning to realize it. What specifically is the trouble?"

"I can't be specific about any one thing. Everything down there is plumb worn out—the generators, the compressors, and so far as I can tell, the main engine."

"Well, I haven't finished my deck inspection yet—probably won't for a couple of weeks, but I haven't yet found anything brand new. We'll just have to do the best we can."

After Ka-Leut left the cabin, he added:

"I don't know what shape she'll be in when we leave here, but she's sure a bucket of bolts now."

Chapter IV

The ship was built to carry 220 cadets, 125 enlisted men, and fourteen officers. The designers had deliberately worked toward the end of making maximum use of muscles, rather than machinery. To get up anchor required two teams of twenty men each, one team hoisting while the other rested. An opportunity to use muscles was the only thing furnished for the hoisting of her boats, for her braces, sheets, inhauls, outhauls and halyards.

In sharp contrast to this ancient mariner setup, certain parts of the vessel are well within the electronic age. The ship was fitted throughout with a dial telephone system, with hundreds of relays and delicately arranged circuits. American ship operating methods would never stand for a station bill requiring so many technicians and maintenance personnel for fancy fripperies.

The first three skippers of the *Horst Wessel* were admirals, since this had been the flagship of the training squadron. As a result, the cabin country is a lush area, the likes of which would not be seen on an ordinary man-of-war. The cabin area consists of an entrance passageway, a large cloak room complete with mirror and dressing bench, a pantry, cabin office lined in mahogany, a bedroom of rippling golden satinwood, a tiled bathroom with a large old-fashioned tub on legs, and a dining saloon paneled in mahogany.

The wardroom resembles an intimate night club. Dining niches are done in natural oak and red leather. The overhead lighting is indirect and rheostat controlled. There were no warrant officers in the German Navy, but the chief petty officers occupied a position slightly higher in the service scale than do similar ratings in our service. The CPO's had their own wardroom and individual staterooms, together with pantry and messboys. Their wardroom was handsomely decorated with oil paintings.

The first and second class petty officers also had their own separate mess and pantry, on a more modest scale.

Measured against the background of the officers' quarters, the German seaman led a Spartan existence. His quarters were open and empty, except for a row of hammock hooks along opposing bulkheads. A German seaman had constantly before him concrete evidence of the material rewards which accompanied promotion.

The ship's galley was surprisingly small. The cookstove was almost a miniature. It was dwarfed by two enormous steam kettles. The whole thing appeared inadequate to take care of the needs of such a large complement.

The more I explored this vessel, the more fascinated I became with her complex arrangement. Going from bow to stern, one encounters seven distinct areas that can be isolated as a damage control measure. Her watertight doors are of battleship caliber, of the rack-and-pinion sliding type, with steel wedge sealing. In four of the bulkheads watertight integrity is complete, with no penetration, making it necessary to go up-and-over in order to get into the adjoining compartment.

She had a barber shop, a tailor shop, a generous sail locker, big enough to lay out and work on her largest courses. There was a soft drink manufacturing plant, equipped with carbonating and bottling machine and ice-cream maker. Plenty of space was set aside for wine lockers against the rigors of long cruises and visits of state in foreign ports.

The conditions prescribed by the Allies in the turning over of the *Horst Wessel* to the United States required, among other things, that the ship should be made in all respects seaworthy at no cost to the American Government. This meant all sail cloth, spare parts and fittings must come from German establishments. New sails had to be produced in German sail lofts by German sailmakers.

Sail cloth now in use on square-rigged sailing ships is made of flax, this being considered more suitable than cotton duck, since it does not get as hard and stiff when wet, but is still one of the strongest known vegetable fibers. This is a concession to the fact that the days of the horny-handed square-riggerman who spits to windward is a thing of the past. The square-rigged ships now in use in northern European countries serve as the young man's introduction to the sea, and since modern mechanization does not permit long periods of time to be devoted to this one phase of a sailor's education, the use of this softer material is necessary. It would have been a simple matter to buy the cloth in London, Copenhagen or Stockholm, but the use of dollars, pounds or kroner was forbidden.

The problem of obtaining suitable sails in sufficient number loomed larger as the days went by. Sail cloth appeared to be almost non-existent. Time after time the supply officer was sent by jeep to some part of Germany on a hot lead, only to receive the discouraging news that the warehouse which had been the "target for the day" had previously been the target of allied bombers. We had so many disappointments that I began to develop a persecution complex. This was partly eased by a 'phone call from the Military Governor's office in Berlin.

"Hello, McGowan, are you there? This is Colonel Blank. I have some good news for you, which I will confirm by dispatch. We have heard that you had to have sail cloth and I have found some in the records of captured material. Send a representative to Kassel and tell him to go to warehouse

56

No. 32. The local MP's will point it out. About how much do you need?"

"Offhand, Colonel, I would say about 3000 yards in standard width of the various weights."

"OK, we will authorize some extra for good measure, say 8000 yards, or let's make it meters—that's the way it's listed here. Then you can take some spare stuff home."

"That's wonderful, Colonel. That's the best news I've had since we got here. I wish it were all as good as this."

"Well, fine. I'm glad we can help you. If there's anything else we can do, be sure to call us."

"Thank you, sir."

Elated, I hung up. This was too good to be true!

Three days later my supply officer came in from Kassel, his shoulders sagging with dejection.

"What's the matter, man? Couldn't you find the warehouse?"

"I found it all right, Cap'n, and make no mistake about it, I found the right one. There was nothing but four walls and some rubble. That warehouse was hit and burned in an air raid over a year ago. What those jokers in Berlin did was to pick up a piece of paper and read from it."

So—I was the winner of 8000 yards of ashes.

The main engine was slated for a minor inspection and a routine replacement of visibly worn parts, *if* we could get the parts. After mulling the conversation with Ka-Leut over in my mind, I decided, in the face of 6000 hours of operation, that it would be foolish to overlook this opportunity to find out all about the engine. Early one morning I ordered a complete pulldown and a searching inspection of the entire engine.

Just before noon my chief machinist's mate, without the customary knock, unceremoniously burst into the cabin.

"You better come down to the engine room, Cap'n. That engine looks like a total loss."

57

With dread, I approached the dismantled engine. At first I could see nothing wrong, and glanced around indignantly at the black gang for giving me such a fright. Every face wore a look of such grave concern that I knew this was no gag. Then I saw it. With the feeling of discovering a mottled snake coiled in tangled underbrush, I made out a spidery, almost invisible crack extending from the wall of No. 2 cylinder to No. 3, skipping to the other wall of No. 3 through to No. 4, and from 4 to 5, and 5 to 6, and 6 to 7. This hunk of steel was being held together by the bolts which fastened down the cylinder head assemblies. Only a matter of time underway, maybe ten hours, perhaps five minutes, lay between almost normal operation and a totally disabling breakdown.

Without a word, I turned and left the engine room.

First no sails; now no engine. Given the sails, it would be possible for a better man than I to get the ship back without the main engine, but a better man just wasn't handy for the job. To get back with any kind of luck and within a reasonable time, that engine had to run to get the ship in and out of harbors and to take up some of the slack when the breeze failed.

Name plate data revealed that the engine had been produced by the M.A.N. factory in Augsburg. The harried supply officer was dispatched to Augsburg. He returned with the news that the Augsburg factory, although in the American zone, had been turned over to the British, who were using its output in support of their urgent mine sweeping program in the North Sea. Faced with this new crisis, I jumped into my car and drove to British Navy Headquarters in Hamburg for a hat-in-hand interview with the Commodore.

Upon entering his office, I noted a distinct chill in the air. The Commodore appeared to be well past sixty. Barely acknowledging our introduction, he peered at me through

58

frigid blue eyes. A pair of horn-rimmed glasses skidded down toward the tip of his nose. He took my measure while I squirmed inwardly. The cool reception and the level wordless stare had the desired effect of intimidation. I had the feeling that anything I might say would certainly sound idiotic. I went completely on the defensive as he casually picked me to pieces with questions. It was obvious that the Yanks weren't going to get a damn thing at the expense of the precious mine-sweeping program. I felt that I had my answer wrapped up in a neat package before I had even made my request. When I finally blurted out my proposition, a new engine block from his factory, he fell silent. I supposed he was composing some Noel Cowardish answer.

The Commodore's gaze fastened upon the gold shield on my sleeve. His expression changed.

"I say, Coast Guard, are you?"

I admitted it.

Whereupon, he called in a stenographer and dictated a letter authorizing free access to the Augsburg factory, and gave me assurance that we could have "any bleddy thing" we wanted.

"The Coast Guard's no stranger to me, y'know. I rode one of your stout little craft here and there in the channel on 'D' day. Picked up dozens of flyers swimming about. Coast Guard chap got decorated. Damn fine show. Met other Coast Guard vessels before and after 'D' day. They were smart vessels. Glad to help with the *Horst Wessel* if she's for your branch.

"My dear chap, you must let us give you lunch. Terribly sorry I cawn't be there. Must dash off to Cuxhaven. I'm the great loser, y'know. Would love to sit and talk Coast Guard."

He rang for an orderly.

"Take this gentleman down to the senior officers' mess.

59

Tell Captain Brown for me that he is Coast Guard and that it is my express desire that the drinks shall be on me."

With a pat on my shoulder, he dashed out.

The mission was a success. To have my outfit recognized for what it was put the frosting on the cake. This was the first time since I had been in Europe that I hadn't had to explain to someone what the U. S. Coast Guard was and what I was doing there. On the few times that I had not been almost invariably accepted as just another naval officer, I had been mistaken for a merchant marine officer, a theatre doorman, and a railroad conductor, even by people in the American armed forces. To be singled out by a Britisher seemed a special sort of thing. I felt warm inside, even before the genial captain I met greeted me with an extended hand which held a Scotch and soda.

Back in Bremen, the engine crisis, if not completely solved, at least on the way to a happy outcome, I turned my attention to other matters. I had picked up a rumor that the navy had custody of a big warehouse, perhaps not empty, near Columbus Key. So I barreled off in that direction.

The Key itself is an old berthing spot for the liners *Bremen* and *Europa,* and was a familiar sight to many an American prewar tourist. Because the Key area was undamaged it provided a usable seaport for deep draft vessels. The Allies had agreed to the creation of the Bremen Enclave. This was a fifty mile wide patch of real estate, roughly the shape of an oak leaf, which was declared American Zone, completely surrounded by the British Zone of occupation. This allowed the Americans to have access to a major port for the embarkation of troops and a flow of supplies for the occupation forces.

The waterfront area was enclosed in barbed wire and guarded by Military Police. This was a hopeful sign. Perhaps I could mooch around and legally scrounge something

60

or other for the ship. Near the Key I came to a big stone warehouse. The German watchman cheerfully produced the keys and escorted me in.

With all the windows shuttered, the interior of the lower floor was almost completely dark. I stood a while, waiting for my eyes to adjust to the gloom. Yanking out a handkerchief, I polished my glasses. Faintly at first, bulky objects began to appear. Row upon row of coils of rope materialized. I approached a coil and picked up a loose end protruding from the top. Here before me lay a five foot thick coil of new five-inch Manila line, the exact thing so badly needed to replace the tattered tacks and sheets of the lower courses of the *Horst Wessel*. A surge of excitement mushroomed inside me. There beyond lay another coil and another! They extended down an aisle that looked as long as a football field. Most of the coils were neatly stitched up in burlap covers and had obviously never been opened.

Afraid the lode would run out, I scampered over to the next row. There more good fortune awaited. On this row the rope was a size smaller—just what we needed for the stuff higher up. I ordered the watchman to open a few windows in order to get a better look at my bonanza. It turned out better than my wildest hopes. There was plenty of all sizes—more than we could possibly jam into the holds as spare loot. There were even gigantic rolls of eight- and ten-inch hawser, but this would be of little use to the *Horst Wessel* since we did not expect to do any towing. At the end of World War II U. S. seagoing personnel had learned to limit the use of Manila line to a bare minimum, since the war in the Pacific had cut off the supply and made it worth its weight in gold.

The watchman seemed to share my enthusiasm. "Ve got more." He led me to the basement. There he showed me thousands of items, all specifically designed for shipboard use. There were bins full of shiny new marlinspikes; there were fids and mallets, turnbuckles, spectacle irons, a generous supply of oakum, tarred hemp of all sizes, and a million wire rope clamps, bolts and shackles. This was a ship rigger's dream.

After wallowing about in my newly found bed of mariner's catnip, I had the watchman seal up the building. On the way back to the ship I stopped in to call on my boss at the Base. With elaborate nonchalance I sidled up to the subject:

"Commodore, may I have a free hand in rounding up stuff necessary for the fitting out of the *Horst Wessel?*"

"Why, yes, McGowan; anybody interfering?"

"No, sir. I think, considering the *Horst Wessel's* rig, I ought to have some sort of priority when I discover stuff, seeing as how it's going to be so hard to find things we must have. For instance, one of my officers has whipped out a slide rule and estimated that we need twenty-two miles of line just to replace worn out stuff; and to call the ship seaworthy, there ought to be an ample supply in the bosun's locker and hawser room."

"As much as that?"

"Well, it may not be exact, but it's beginning to look like it will take that much."

"You have a free hand. Take anything you can find within reason. Good hunting!"

"It's all right then if I pass this word to the supply officer?"

"Yes, it is."

With remarkable self-restraint I drifted over to the supply office and relayed the message. After I got my car out of sight of Headquarters I roared back to the ship. I called my officers together, broke the good news, and ordered every inch of running rigging renewed before sailing day, and all possible space down below loaded with this beautiful new cordage and gear.

My supply officer was born in Germany and brought to America when he was twelve years old. His forays across Germany brought him into daily contact with his former countrymen, and his ability to speak German soon came back to him. He was frequently mistaken for a German official by the townspeople. One day I overheard one of the villagers addressing him as "Graf" (Count). It would be interesting to know what Von, in his fluent German, was telling these people about himself. In any case, "Graf" Von's assignment to my detail was a stroke of luck.

At first I undertook to direct his movements by assigning him to go to a particular place and look for a special thing, but it was not long in dawning that I was wasting both my own time and his. This treasure hunt had to be an independently conducted job for an opportunist. We agreed that the rest of us would provide Von with a basic list of needed items, which could be revised from time to time. He was then given freedom to roam wherever he chose, grabbing whatever he found, using any expedient at hand, and no questions asked. He made many unexplained trips, and stuff began to roll in. Sometimes it would be reduced to a trickle. Occasionally he would hit the jackpot.

In Von's zeal, he continued to unearth things we might *just possibly* need, until we were burdened with an embarrassment of riches. He persisted in the search for sail cloth and located an enormous store of the stuff in a town many miles inland. After he had achieved the impossible by finding a grand total of 9000 meters, we were still without sail twine. Undaunted, he hit the trail on the new search, and within a week had found more twine than could be used by the ship for years to come.

The Weser River estuary faces the North Sea. Winter and early spring months in this area bring foul weather. It seemed that the sun would never shine. The temperature hovered around the freezing mark enough to make life miserable. When it was above freezing the snow and ice turned to slush and mud. One howling gale after another came sweeping in from the north. It meant the deferment of work on the topside and the rigging until the weather improved. There was plenty to do indoors, but our means of propulsion—our "main engine"—was aloft.

The bad weather reached indoors. One of my officers went on an inspection trip to Hamburg where the new sails were being made. He reported that the sail lofts were unheated and the sailmakers, blue with cold and weak from lack of food, were getting nothing done. Von made a furtive trip to Hamburg with a truckload of food. The workers also got a mysterious windfall of fuel for their stoves.

After our help to the sailmakers, the boss man got into the act. The sails were to be produced by a syndicate, or guild, of five sail-making firms. One morning Ka-Leut told me that the head of the sailmakers' firms wanted an interview. He professed to speak no English, but had a prolonged conversation with Ka-Leut, who acted as interpreter. His was the painful duty of breaking more bad news. He was blushing like a schoolgirl.

The upshot of the conversation was that the sailmaking firms wanted double the amount of sail cloth necessary for the new sails. This would enable them to continue in the sailmaking business after completing my job, showing a neat one hundred percent profit. I got the story by inference and deduction, since Ka-Leut was unwilling to translate this piece of attempted brigandage verbatim. The rascal got a non-committal postponement of decision as an answer. Obviously he had heard about our big haul.

That night I looked up a Colonel in Military Government. Somewhere along the line we had exchanged a favor or two and were on very friendly terms.

"Got anything to do tonight?"

"No, Mac. I just got off a letter to my wife. Glad you came in. I was feeling lonely."

"Come on over to my joint and I'll pour you a drink."

"Good idea. Let's go."

I carefully avoided the subject of my ship's business until he was thoroughly mellowed. We talked of various things until he finally walked into it without suspecting that the thing was being engineered.

"By the way, how's the *Horst Wessel* coming?"

"Just fine—can't complain. My split engine block is going to be replaced, and Von made a terrific strike a couple of weeks ago by discovering all the sail cloth we need. We let a contract with the sailmakers' guild in Hamburg, so it looks like we've about got that angle licked too. You know, a funny thing happened today. The boss of the sailmakers' guild came over here to see me. The son-of-a-gun wanted practically our entire stock of cloth as a sort of dividend payment for making the sails."

The Colonel sat bolt upright.

"What did you tell the buzzard?"

"Oh, I stalled him. Frankly, I didn't know what to say. I have a sneaking feeling of sympathy for the guy when you look at the thing from his point of view. At the same time, this job has gotta be done, and I'd hate to see those guys sabotage the job just by dragging their feet and claiming they weren't able to finish. I'd be tempted to meet his proposition out of ordinary humanity so the dozens of sailmakers involved would have a means of livelihood guaranteed after they finish this job. The hard facts of life are that this batch of cloth we have is only enough to meet our needs, with a little left over for the *Albert Schlageter* when the time comes to fit her out. There must be more of the cloth hidden here and there in Germany, and those birds will eventually get their hands on it."

"Leave everything to me, Mac. Those crooks are being

paid at our order by the burgomeister in German marks, and charged to war reparations. Don't waste your sympathy on them. They are being treated fairly, and have made a dangerous proposition so far as they are concerned. They could land in jail. I'm going to Hamburg tomorrow. It just happens that I know this clown you're talking about. I'll throw such a scare into him that you'll hear no more about the matter."

There were no more calls from Hamburg and no more demands for sail cloth.

One of the jobs tackled in the early stages was the removal of ballast from the "washwasser" tank for a thorough cleaning, in order to provide more drinking water. The ship carried most of her ballast in the two central tanks. It was made up of ninety-pound pigs of iron, stacked and wedged in the inboard sections of the tanks. Just as I had surmised, over a period of years the spaces between the pieces of ballast had accumulated fouling to a point where the water was constantly polluted. To remove the ballast it had to be lifted by hand through the tank top and carried aft along the passageway about twenty feet before being hoisted through the hatch on the topside.

Three or four days after the removal order, almost nothing had been accomplished. I took the matter up with Ka-Leut. When I asked him about the progress, I could tell from his quick answer that he had been expecting the question. He was a close friend of the yard owner, and had been in a huddle with him about this very problem.

"That is a most difficult job, Cap-tain. You see, the ship is built in a peculiar fashion around those tank tops."

We leaned over the table and examined the ship's hull plans together.

"It looks all right to me, Ka-Leut. It's a little awkward that the ballast has to be carried by hand along a passage

66

before you can use a tackle, but there appears to be plenty of room."

"Yes, sir. I must tell the truth. These yard workmen are very weak. They are not strong enough to lift the ballast pigs. They have very little food these days."

I had heard that the official government ration in Hamburg was 1100 calories per person per day, which is not-so-slow starvation. I did not know precisely how scarce the food was in Bremerhaven, but it did occur to me that the workmen were a gaunt looking lot. The hang of their clothes suggested that scarecrows were repairing the *Horst Wessel*.

After pondering the matter, I decided to postpone the removal of the ballast. All I wanted was a clean tank temporarily. The solution was to pour cement over the ballast until we got a firm seal which would isolate the pollution. This makeshift would suit our purposes until the ship could be overhauled in an American shipyard. It was so ordered.

My boys were impressed with the Germans' willingness to work. They became sympathetic with the plight of these men who were trying so hard and accomplishing so little. Spontaneously, food began to disappear in small bits here and there from the American mess hall. After that, our scarecrows began to fill out and the work went ahead a little faster. Maybe it was my clear duty to investigate these petty thefts, but I looked the other way.

Chapter V

Six weeks after we, the advance guard, landed in Germany, the second American group arrived by ship. They brought news of what had been happening in the States. Demobilization was in full swing. With the Coast Guard being cut back to prewar strength by June 30th, it was clear that we would not get sufficient manpower from America to sail the ship home safely. In this group, along with the new executive officer and an electrical engineering specialist, were downy-cheeked apprentice seamen, many of whom had never been to sea before. This addition brought the total manpower to about fifty.

On running through a copy of the orders, I found that the seamen were all beginners. They were the most recent crop from boot camp. I suppose what I did next was a bit corny. I had the group assemble in the Base chapel, and took my position before them in the spot ordinarily occupied by the chaplain on Sunday morning.

It is customary in the service when a new skipper takes over for him to get up in front of his new crew and make a few remarks. The remarks are usually a few statements to the effect that "We live by the book;" "You are a fine looking crew;" "This is a splendid ship and we intend to keep her so;" etc. This time they were not yet a crew and ship commissioning was in the distant future, but I believed that I owed it to these youngsters to try to get across to them a few facts of life while they were getting their first impressions of their new surroundings.

"I am your new commanding officer. I brought you here because I wanted a little privacy for what I have to say to you. It is possible that this is the first trip away from home for most of you, and I would say it's a cinch that you haven't been to Germany before. I've been here six weeks and I think I've got the situation sized up pretty well.

"Make no mistake about it, what you do over here is going to be watched closely and it's going to be talked about. While you are here I want you never to lose sight of the fact that you are Coastguardsmen. You may have found out already that damn few people know what the Coast Guard is and still fewer know what it does. You are on a job that has never been done before by the Coast Guard, and because of this, people are going to take special interest in you.

"I suppose you've heard of the candy bar circuit. I couldn't ride herd on you and shoo away the fraulines if I wanted to, but I want you to remember that there are two kinds—daughters of respectable German families who almost never let them out of the house and would disown them if they caught them talking to a foreigner; and there is the other kind that walk the streets. These will speak to you without being whistled at, and in most cases they will proposition you. A Navy doctor lives in the same billet I do, and I have learned plenty from him about what's been happening to the troops over here. A company of truck drivers is billeted near where I live. The doctor tells me that their VD incidence rate in one year was 400 per cent.

"For those of you who haven't had this job explained, I think this is a good time to tell you something about the ship. She's a three-masted bark, 295 feet long, and she's all hand powered on the topside. You're going to find out what the word 'handpower' means in a big way before the trip is over, but we're going to try to run things so no one will suffer from overwork.

"You've got an opportunity here to get to know more seamanship in a short time than any of the petty officers
69

who taught you in boot camp. When you get back to the States you're going to be sought after as qualified able-bodied seamen. In my opinion, you should make the best petty officers the service has known for many years. The opportunity is here for you. I'm going to work hell out of you, and then I'm going to reward you as best I can with liberty in good clean places like Madeira and Bermuda, possibly St. Thomas and Miami.

"Take a look around and you'll see that liberty here in Germany is not going to offer much more than an opportunity to look at some awful ruins. There are no night clubs, no cafés, you can't buy any food ashore. There aren't any souvenirs worth having except those you will find in the ship's store. There you'll find French perfume and some very nice things that come from Switzerland.

"To get back to the subject of the Coast Guard—you men are the official representatives of the entire service, this handful of you, and there'll be about six hundred Navy men around comparing you with themselves. This is one time when I want the Navy to come off second best.

"When you get to the ship, study the rigging all the time. Your life may depend upon your knowledge of which line to grab and which to keep your hands off while you are aloft. That is all. The chief will show you to your new quarters."

Just at this time a letter from the Academy told me that the deal was off—the cadets weren't coming. Shortage of manpower at the Academy was putting added burdens on the student body. The Washington people were too preoccupied with problems of their own to give any further thought to the future of the *Eagle*. With no authorization to employ Germans, and with too few American hands to work the ship safely, it began to look as though the project was doomed to failure. There was nothing to do but carry on and hope for the best. I consoled myself with the

70

"Study the rigging all the time."

"Your life will depend on your knowledge of which line to grab when you are aloft."

thought that any change from now on would be for the better, and that somehow, something would turn up to make it possible to get the ship home.

Taking stock of the situation only made things seem blacker. The skipper was a green hand in square-riggers. The executive officer, an excellent seaman, was limited in experience to small boat sailing. The two junior officers had much the same background. The engineer officer was primarily a steam man, whereas all machinery down below was diesel; the deck force green hands. We were blessed with two excellent boatswain's mates, one of whom had sailed in commercial fishermen but never in square-riggers. That was the debit side.

Our assets were nebulous. We were in good health; we were learning; we had grown very fond of this vessel with her beautiful lines.

As the situation worsened, the weather improved. When the tulips began to pop out and splashes of green to soften the jagged contours of the ruined areas, our troubles multiplied.

Von got back from Augsburg ahead of the new engine block. He was cocky with success.

"There was nothing to it. Everything went like a breeze. I just showed them the Limey Commodore's letter and from then on I was a V I P. We went right down to the assembly line and earmarked a block, and it's on its way. Should be here by tomorrow."

"The thing must weigh two or three tons. How about the transportation?"

"It's coming on a ten-wheel flat bed trailer. The Army was very good about it when they saw my liquor supply."

I went to the topside and, for the first time, began to wonder how the block was going to get into the engine room when the double skylight hatches were only about two feet wide and three feet long. I walked 'round and 'round the engine room trunk looking for an opening big enough to accommodate this hunk of steel, and there wasn't any.

Ka-Leut came up.

"You hear about our new block?"

"Yes, Cap-tain, that is fine news."

"How are we going to get it in the ship?"

He pointed to a row of hexagonal bolt heads running along the edge of the deck around the entire engine room trunk.

"Those bolts come up and the whole cover lifts off like the top of a coffee can. The workmen are getting ready to take the old block out now. Here comes the schwim-crain."

The floating crane from another part of the yard rounded the corner of the slip astern of us as he spoke. It was being chuff-chuffed in our direction by an ancient tug with a tall skinny stack. With consummate skill the tug pilot swung the crane alongside us, stopping just inches from the side, and made an eggshell landing. Our crew made the lines fast and the crane head swung over the engine room, ready for hoisting.

While this was in progress, the workmen had been breaking the ancient layers of paint away from the bolt heads, and with mighty heaves were starting the bolts. Some of them were so badly rusted into place that the heads snapped off. At any rate, the skylight pieces were ready for hoisting in a fairly short time. As the big cover was swung away, more engineering ingenuity in construction came to light. All the frames, pipelines, and wiring were routed in such a way as to make a clear vertical lift possible directly over the engine. To move the block still required a lot of know-how, because it had to be tilted and lifted at the same time, in order to clear the narrow limits of this access hole in the deck. This took a lot of maneuvering of the various wire rope leads of the hoisting gear.

74

As the block came to rest on the deck of the crane, I climbed down to have a last look at the crack which had given us so much grief. Now that we had the trouble cured, the thing had lost its sinister appearance and looked like an innocent little line connecting the cylinder holes from end to end.

Next morning the new block arrived. Setting it down on the old engine bed was simply a reverse procedure of what had happened the day before. To witness the ceremony I climbed down into the engine room. As our prize was gently lowered and canted into place, I lit a flash light to get a clear view. With the block hovering over the engine bed only a few inches more to go, I blinked to get rid of what looked like an optical illusion. Just as in the comic gag, where there is an extra buttonhole at the top of a vest and an extra button at the bottom, the holding down bolts and the bolt holes weren't lining up properly. This thing just *had* to fit. It was the right serial number, the right mark, the right builder's date; everything checked.

I darted a look at the boss rigger and the yard machinist. Their expressions told me all I needed to know. The damn thing did not fit.

I yelled for Von.

"Come here and look at your prize. What went wrong? Is this the block you so proudly pulled off the assembly line?"

He examined the thing silently for more than a minute.

"It beats hell out of me, Cap'n. That block was checked and double checked, but it sure don't fit."

Sadly we climbed the engine room ladder and went into a huddle on deck.

"Von, I want you to double check every figure on the engine, on the bed, and on the invoice, and take off for Augsburg with your precious letter."

Von lit out for Augsburg without waiting for lunch.

75

When he returned a few days later, he had the solution to the mystery, thanks to having run into a German engineer who had been at the factory since the time the *Horst Wessel* was built. During the war the factory had re-designed the engine without indicating the change with a modification number. He and Von had worked out the solution to our problem. They had compared the engine bed plate and crankshaft bearing measurements. They found that a new bed plate which *would* fit our new block would, at the same time, accommodate our crankshaft and the other fittings in the lower part of our engine.

The new bed plate arrived promptly and the work of assembling our almost new engine went along without a hitch.

Typical of Von, he had managed to scrounge new valve assemblies, and various other parts here and there as dividends. As he was bragging about his successes, I interrupted to say: "This is about the same as jacking up a whistle and running a new ship under it."

"It was about time for us to have a little luck, Cap'n. I was beginning to think you'd be better off if you shipped me home. By the way, Cap'n," his manner became elaborately casual, "On the way home I did some more mooching around and uncovered some stuff that we might be able to use. There were some code and signal flags I latched on to and a few more odds and ends. They're coming in on a German railroad."

Several days later an entire trainload of naval supplies and equipment arrived. By actual count, there were a hundred thousand signal flags. All we could possibly use were two complete alphabets and a few special flags, a total of about seventy-five. There were one thousand dozen marlinspikes of assorted sizes—enough for a thousand ships!

Von's energetic scavenging served an excellent purpose in that it brought widely scattered ship equipment into the hands of people who knew its value and who were able to see that the material was put to proper use. All that we couldn't use was turned over to the Naval Base. There were other ships to be fitted out in Bremerhaven.

We wondered how so much ship's gear got so far inland. A plausible reason was that Germany's submarine building program had been scattered far and wide in sub-assembly projects, thus shortening the period in which main assembly would be concentrated at known shipyards, and consequently under fire by Allied bombers. We heard that small parts of submarines were built back in mountain villages.

With better weather some thought had to be given to a schedule of outside work, wherein the renewal of the rigging would provide training for the new crew. A tentative assignment of sail stations was made, the German sailors being used in key spots where their familiarity with the rigging could best be observed by the green hands. There could be no question of putting a German in a position of authority. After commissioning day the *Eagle* would be a public vessel of the United States, and as such must be commanded entirely by Americans. Ka-Leut understood this. He assisted tirelessly in instructing his men to go through all the operations as graphically as possible for the benefit of the learners.

The first step of the outside work was the opening and inspection of the standing rigging. The standing rigging is made up of those lines which support the masts and yards. This is composed of shrouds and stays. The shrouds are rows of steel wire ropes that lead sharply downward from the mast to the sides of the ship. They are fanned out in such a way that they provide a ready means for the crew to climb to sail stations in the rigging. Short lines lead horizontally from shroud to shroud, forming a spider-web-like ladder. These are ratlines. Renewing the ratlines on a ship is "rattling down," a briny expression. The shrouds pro-

77

vide athwartship bracing for the mast, and the stays support the mast in a fore and aft direction.

The running rigging, consisting of lines that can be hauled and slacked and moved about in various ways, enables the crew to present to the wind the desired sail surfaces whereby the ship gets her push through the water.

The masts of square-riggers and, for that matter, vessels with fore and aft sails, are all raked aft, which means that they lean slightly aft from the vertical. In some vessels the raking of the mast is rather extreme. An example is the "bug eye" rig of the fishermen on Chesapeake Bay. The raking has a two-fold purpose. It allows a tall mast to carry the same sail area as though it were standing vertical, but, at the same time, permits the mast to travel through a shorter arc as the vessel rolls in a seaway. The raking of masts, and on modern steamships, the funnels, presents a pleasanter silhouette than if masts and stacks stood starkly upright. On a sailing ship it serves a more important purpose. It makes it possible to gain added strength because most of the strain from the pressure of wind on the sails is from aft moving the ship forward on its course.

The stays that lead forward and downward from the various masts are usually very light, and give rise to a common expression in the language which has come ashore from the sea and joined the vocabularies of landsmen. When a ship is "caught aback," she has been placed in a dangerous situation either by inept handling or by the sudden reversal of wind direction which sometimes occurs in connection with unstable, squally weather. A square-rigger is caught aback when she has come into the wind, causing all the squares'ls to be pressing back against the masts and yards. If the pressure is great enough, releasing the halyards and downhauls is ineffective and the sails and yards remain glued into place, putting exceptional strain on the forward leading stays. The damage which may result

78

Working on the rigging in sunny weather.

Renewing the ratlines is called "rattling down."

A well ordered arrangement of infinitely complex sea-going "furni-ture."

can range from the loss of one or more masts to the loss of the vessel.

The *Danmark* was caught aback in the middle of a squally night while rounding into the North Sea north of Scotland on her way home in 1945. There a green helmsman unconsciously followed his lubber's line up into the wind while the officer of the deck had gone forward for a moment to check on the men at the jibs.

Following the lubber's line is a mistake common to an inexperienced helmsman. As he stands at the wheel gazing at the compass card, he sees on the border of the card a point or a number which has been designated as his course. Just beyond the card is a vertical black line on the rim of the compass, or in some cases, a pin extending out over the edge of the card. This pin, or line, is called the "lubber's line," and represents the exact center line of the ship. As the ship's head moves to the right, the lubber's line moves to the right along the edge of the compass; and as a result, the compass card appears to be turning to the left. Since the compass card is pointing steadily north magnetic, this apparent movement of the card is an optical illusion. The green hand will put the wheel to the right, which will only turn the ship's head faster to the right. Unless the apprentice is corrected, he will chase his line and the ship around in a tight circle.

The OD discovered the condition after it was too late, and as he dashed aft he threw lines off the belaying pins, hoping that some of the straining gear aloft would feel this easing of tension and would slide down automatically, but the pressure was so great that the sails remained glued in place while the peril mounted.

The captain was roused from his bunk as he felt the ship suddenly go upright from her normal heeled over position on the starboard tack, and needed no messenger to bring him to the quarterdeck on a dead run. He put the wheel over to a full right position, and prayed. As the ship gathered sternway she began to feel the rudder and started very slowly falling off the wind. With all hands tensely waiting for the first stay to part, the ship snapped around in a swiftly rising crescendo of roaring gear as the sails and yards came unstuck. Lines leaped about the deck like maddened serpents, and sparks twinkled aloft as metal parts clashed against metal, and yards snapped topping lifts taut until they twanged like guitar strings.

This second-hand account, relayed in a heavy Danish accent liberally salted and peppered with devout blasphemy, made me especially attentive as I inspected the fittings and splices of the stays and shrouds.

The ship was being overhauled at Rickmers' Werft, a place familiar to ship riggers, carpenters and sail makers for many years, but now more frequented by boiler makers, welders and pipe fitters. Herr Rickmers was of the fifth generation operating on the same spot. The family had owned a yard in Hamburg, but in view of the damage to both yards, young Herr Rickmers was concentrating all his energy to the salvation of the yard in Bremerhaven as a first step in a desperate effort to revive the name of Rickmers on the high seas.

The young owner was a dark, wiry, intense man. He stood about five feet seven in a pair of shabby sea boots, which were constantly caked with mud and grime. His shiny, faded blue serge suit stood out in immaculate contrast to his foot gear. How he slogged around the muddy yard and climbed through the tangled wreckage without soiling his clothes was a mystery. His faultless courtesy and perfectly enunciated Oxford English erected an invisible barrier between Rickmers, the man, and Rickmers, the ship builder, hell-bent upon getting a difficult job done against terrible odds. The level stare of his deep brown eyes and the stainless steel polish of his speech transmitted only

82

facts and figures. I could find not a trace of emotion in his voice. As he ended a conversation and went about his business, I subconsciously listened for the sound of clicking heels. I determined to get to know this man, and if possible, break down some of his reserve. I went out of my way to be friendly and offered to meet the guy halfway, but seemed to be making no headway in establishing any warmer ties than those one might have with an adding machine.

One day, as was his custom, he sent his secretary on board to arrange for an interview. After this bit of formality, I was prepared to discuss more problems of ship's work. When he entered the cabin he looked his normal ramrod self. He spoke in his usual deadpan manner:

"Captain, I was fortunate enough to salvage some rather special wines after the bombing of Hamburg. I inherited most of them from my father and had them buried in the ground. Would you be good enough to join me in my office tonight at seven?"

"I will be glad to come, Herr Rickmers."

"Thank you, sir."

Without a change of expression he bowed slightly and went ashore.

That night I arrived at the appointed hour and was received in his usual manner. His office was a partitioned off end of a single story warehouse, but had the luxury of clean concrete floor and faded green window shades. The place was painfully neat, and aside from the two desks, single typewriter and three straight chairs, as bare as the cellar of a vacant house. This was also Herr Rickmers' home. He slept on a folding army cot behind a partition adjoining the office. Where and what he ate I never knew.

"I thought you might be interested in helping me sample these wines. The corks are firm and they appear to be in decent condition. I suggest that we start with the light

83

ones, then each heavier grade can be appreciated for itself and not be obscured by too much weight beforehand."

There was a knock at the door. At Rickmers' "Herein!" the door swung open to admit Ka-Leut. His manner was easy and relaxed. He had shed his customary shipboard correctness and, for the first time, I saw him as a man among friends. He ambled across the room and slouched into a chair.

With a casual nod to Ka-Leut, Herr Rickmers produced three crystal wine glasses, whose facets twinkled, reflecting the light of the naked bulb suspended overhead by a twisted green cord. A row of bottles stood along the center line of a flat desk top, their labels barely decipherable through age and exposure. Rickmers had carefully pasted white squares of paper on the shoulder of every bottle. Each square was numbered. Corkscrew in hand, he reached for bottle number one. It was a delicate white still wine, with only a hint of amber coloring.

I was brought up in the era of Prohibition and my wine tasting education neglected. In spite of thirteen years of legal samplings, I am still an illiterate among connoisseurs when it comes to vintages. Nevertheless, the quality of these wines, as we progressed from bottle to bottle, impressed me as something special. We sipped the wine leisurely and talked. Rickmers and Ka-Leut stuck strictly to English throughout the evening and discussed such things as bouquet, and aftertaste, and character among wines. The conversation came around to shipbuilding and the exploits of the Kaiser interests during the war. I became aware of a subtle change in Rickmers' manner. He began to address me as a person.

"You know, we ship builders were very well informed about what was going on in the States in ship building, and Mr. Kaiser's 'put-a-ship-together-in-four-days' worried us not at all in the beginning. German Intelligence was so

84

complete that we could analyze American ship building progress down to fractions in terms of cost per ton, man hours per ton, and total production per month; and matching them up against our U-boat activity which was taking away so many tons per month, we laughed and joked about how far we were ahead of you. Then came a turning point that we knew about before the German military. When Mr. Kaiser reached a point where he used fewer man hours per ton than we did, we knew the jig was up. We were working at a strained maximum capacity, but we were losing the race. We knew this even before the massive raids finished the job."

As he talked his eyes sparkled; his expression became animated. Occasionally he smiled. The wine had helped to crack the glacial façade, but it was not the wine alone. In the privacy of his office, Herr Rickmers became a friendly fellow.

We fell to shop talking. Rickmers spoke:

"I think they are going to take the *Horst Wessel* away from me."

"Why?" from me.

"Your Navy is beginning to wonder if we are capable of finishing the job in a reasonable time."

He gestured toward the window. The dull glow of a waning moon silhouetted the grotesque, gnarled features of wreckage against the sky.

"I am surprised that you are able to get anything done."

"We are getting this job done because we must. If they take this away from us it will be the end of the Rickmers Line forever. I am the last of the line. I am not going to fail."

His eyes blazing, he pounded the words out on the top of the desk with his fist, and his voice rose to a shout. He quickly recovered, and very softly said:

"I apologize. I care too much."

I could think of nothing to say.

It occurred to me that his invitation might have been designed to influence the Americans to leave the *Horst Wessel* job with him. But considering the fact that he was on friendly terms with naval officers who were my seniors and who had more control over the allocation of work than I did, I discarded the notion.

We moved from the medium white wines to the light rosy reds. In view of the amount we consumed, and the measure of sanity which remained in evidence in our conversation, I am convinced that the alcholic content was extremely light. Along about eleven o'clock it occurred to me that the wine was having a much greater effect on my two German friends than on me. Their undernourished condition made them easy targets for anything alcoholic. In a downright rosy mood we left the office and picked our way around stacks of rubble to the shipyard gate, where Ducky had previously agreed to pick me up.

Ducky was late and we took refuge from the evening's chill in a glass enclosed watchman's cubicle by the gate. As we stood around a tiny stove, Herr Rickmers picked up a late evening paper and idly scanned the headlines. Suddenly his interest was riveted to a small article on the lower part of the page. He began to tremble with rage, and cursed in English under his breath. He put his head down on his crossed arms on the table top and broke into hard, convulsive sobs.

I caught Ka-Leut's eye, and nodded toward the door. We tiptoed out. As I gently closed the door, I caught the words:

"These damn people will never learn! Time after time Germany tries to destroy herself."

"What's the matter with him, Ka-Leut?"

"It was the newspaper. There was an article about a

revival of the Nazi party. Some people are trying to start 'Der Parti' again."

Ducky rolled up in his Opel.

"Auf Weidersehen, Herr Ka-Leut."

"Auf Weidersehen."

Chapter VI

While the work of fitting out was in progress there were many interested visitors. The majority were would-be sailors. Their display of "sea lore" lifted my morale somewhat. At least, *I* knew more about this business than some. The genuine square-rigger sailormen, though few, were a source of embarrassment. They were keenly interested in the ship and wanted to discuss at length different aspects of the job. I wanted anything but a discussion which would reveal the shakiness of my background.

One of the sharpies was a venerable Scotsman of the Royal Naval Reserve, who was assigned to the Weser River Command as harbormaster at Bremerhaven. He was on active duty as a Commander, although well past retirement age. "Scotty" was a veritable oak of a man. He stood not over five feet nine and weighed upward of two hundred. His rock hard muscles had lost none of their bounce. It was his custom to stomp from his office and through the streets of Bremerhaven the more than three miles to the officers' mess each night after work. The heavy crook-type cane he used to punch out the cadence of his march was a bit of affectation which, I suspect, he thought was appropriate with his snow white hair and craggy weatherbeaten features.

Scotty's route to the mess carried him through an MP check point near the waterfront. Most of the MP personnel knew him by sight, but occasionally a new man on watch would have to satisfy himself as to Scotty's identity. One night a new man halted him and, as most sentries do, casually noted that the photograph on his identification card checked with Scotty's features.

"What is your nationality, sir?"

"I'm a Scot."

"Does that mean you're a Limey, sir?"

"Nope, I'm a Scot."

"What does that mean, sir?"

"It means that I'm a Scot."

Scotty was be damned if he was going to admit to being anything but a native of his beloved homeland. The thundercloud-like scowl on his face might have been a warning to a sensitive man, but a close look would have revealed an evil twinkle in Scotty's eye.

By this time the sentry was bristling with suspicion. His call for re-inforcements brought the officer of the guard on the run. After the impasse was disposed of and Scotty had acknowledged the officer's apology with a curt nod, he marched off toward the mess. If the confused sentry had watched closely, he could have observed Scotty's mighty shoulders heaving in his struggle to suppress his Jovian chuckles.

We met every night at the senior officers' mess and became close friends. I viewed his frequent visits on board the *Eagle* with mixed emotions. Scotty would come up with:

"Mac, what do you think of reefing the fores'l in running before a heavy sea?"

I knew better than to take a stand. Scotty knew the answers to most of his questions before they were asked. He was not trying to pull the rug out from under me; he was simply giving me too much credit and was seeking a lively discussion of a controversial subject. My favorite tactic was to divert the conversation, resolving to secretly find out all I could about reefing fores'ls and re-open the subject later. I learned to pick up things from Scotty by the use of challenging questions of the same nature:

"Scotty, what do you think of the use of harbor gaskets at sea?" (I had read about harbor gaskets the night before.)

Questions began to come in from Washington and New London about the probable sailing date and estimated time of arrival in the U.S. At the end of a day when everything went well I was tempted to make an optimistic prediction. The following morning everything would fall apart.

As long as work was going on in the rigging and machinery parts were being moved from ship to shore and back again, nothing could be done about getting cleaned up or painted. This would be the last stage of work before sailing. The spring weather and the work outdoors had a stimulating effect on the crew. The appearance of new line in the rigging was a symbol of the first faint heart beats of a rebirth. The character of the ship began to change.

The figurehead was a gold eagle with wings outspread, the talons clutching a wreath in which a swastika had been mounted. The "crooked cross" had been removed. I thought it a rare co-incidence that the future *Eagle* should have such a figurehead, but the eagle was simply another piece of Nazi symbolism and appeared everywhere. All training ships had identical devices. The people at home didn't know this, and we planned to point with pride to our masterpiece.

Some days after our wine sampling adventure, Herr Rickmers appeared on deck with a large flat package under his arm.

"Captain, I have here a little token of appreciation for the many courtesies extended by you and your crew."

I could not imagine what the package contained, but thanked him as best I could before tearing off the tissue wrappings. It was a hand-carved piece of teak, the shield which was to replace the swastika on the figurehead. The

90

Our figurehead after the silver shield replaced the Swastika.

silvering had been accomplished by the use of aluminum paint. This final touch made our figurehead complete. This gesture was my proof that he had thawed and that we counted each other as friends.

Another task was the translating of nameplates and the legends on blueprints. With typical thoroughness the Germans had made all the workings of the vessel, above and below, crystal clear to anyone who could read German. Every compartment bore a German legend; every engine part, valve, tank top, pipe line and electrical lead was marked. All those necessary for the homeward passage had to be translated into English, and new name plates manufactured and installed. We were fortunate in getting the services of a former engineer of the North German Lloyd Line. He spent eight hours a day for three months at this arduous task. His work was skillful and accurate, and a great blessing in later days when Americans found the fruits of his labor their only source of information.

The name *Eagle* was not a spur-of-the-moment choice, but is traditional in the Coast Guard. There had been a succession of vessels by this name since the earliest days. When I told Ka-Leut what the ship was to be re-named, he seemed surprised, and chuckled as though I had told a joke. I was puzzled and a little irritated. Realizing that I did not get the point, he sobered.

"Eagle?" he said, and placing his hands about twelve inches apart as if measuring fisherman style, "Eagle? In German that word means little animal, what you call 'groundhog'."

Groundhog!

My friend was thinking in German again.

From my small store of German words I found the one we wanted.

"Oh, no, not 'igel.' 'Eagle' is an English word meaning 'adler'."

92

Comprehension dawned.

"That is a fine name, Cap-tain. It could not be better."

Work to be done on the ship fell into three main divisions. First and most important was the obtaining of the sails and seeing to it that the rigging was in proper condition. Second was the installation of the new engine block, reassembling the main engine and generally putting things in order down below. Third was the scrounging for all the spare parts and gear we could lay hands on. Most of the equipment had no counterpart on the American market. Once the spare parts that we were to bring along were used up, the machine involved would have to be replaced with one of American make. For this reason we became cunning and greedy.

A shining example of irreplaceability was the Anschutz gyro compass. One feature of this fine instrument was that the compass repeater faces could be read with great accuracy from a distance. At a glance, from about ten feet away, I could read the ship's heading within a fifth of a degree. This was a magnificent piece of machinery, but prior to World War II the Germans had tried to keep it off the world market, making it a monopoly for Axis armed vessels. American manufacturers have turned out repeaters of a similar type since the war, but at that time I had not seen anything like the one we had on the *Eagle*.

My electrician's mate was told off to identify all electrical manufacturer's data he could find on shipboard, and to do nothing but scrounge for spare parts on shore. Every day he was out on the prowl to save American taxpayers dollars in years to come. He made a terrific strike in an abandoned boat yard. A small shack concealed a flight of stairs leading underground. Armed with a flashlight and spare batteries, he explored a dank tunnel. Another tunnel, clean and dry, was found behind a lightly fastened door. This, in turn, led him to a complete underground warehouse, where he found thousands and thousands of electrical spare parts of various kinds in near perfect condition.

We heard many stories of such discoveries. The Germans must have been busy as squirrels toward the end of the war, burying stuff they could no longer use, to keep it from falling into the hands of the Allies.

The engine block problem was pretty well solved when Von came back with a new bed plate of the right size. All that remained was the painfully slow assembly job. Everything seemed slow except the passage of time. The days on the calendar slipped by at an alarming rate. In the beginning we had made a rough estimate of the progress of work which could be accomplished from week to week. Shortages, unexpected mechanical failures and fiendish weather laid their sticky hands on the wheels of progress, at times slowing things almost to a dead stop.

With the heavy work nearing completion, the ship was ready for drydocking. Upon entering the dock, the dirt and rubble of the shipyard was left behind. As she settled on the keel blocks and the water receded, her beautiful body was slowly unveiled. She had the underwater lines of a racing yacht, the delicate curving contours of her hull sweeping aft with poetic grace. The Germans beamed with pride, and the Americans' eyes lit up with admiration. This charmer had captured our hearts.

Drydocking a ship is a swift operation. As soon as the water is clear of the hull, gangs of men with high pressure hoses wash away the mud and loose barnacles. This is followed by scraping and wire brushing. The hull was found to be in good condition; no major repairs were necessary except to the rudder. Knowing that the rudder or rudder post or both had been damaged by the near miss bomb, the workmen had provided for a complete rebuilding of the steering gear, if this should be necessary. Fortunately for our schedule, the repair job turned out to be rather

94

simple, and in a few hours the realigned rudder post made it possible to swing the wheel from port to starboard and back with no difficulty.

Since Coast Guard cutters are traditionally white, I wanted the *Eagle* to be the same. Up to now she had been slate gray, with a muddy buff color above the main deck level. The ever-resourceful Von produced the paint—how and from where was his secret. He also found a supply of cleaning gear, soap and brass polish.

Two things of which the crew seemed blissfully unaware nagged at me constantly. The grim fact was that no solution to the manpower problem had occurred to me. News from home, or rather the lack of it, made it plain that no help could be expected from that quarter. My second worry was hurricane season, which sometimes starts as early as June. Unless we got going very soon there was an increasing likelihood of tangling with one before the trip was over.

One Sunday afternoon in late April I was sitting in the naval officers' club indulging in my favorite sport—worry. My feelings must have been reflected in my expression. A British naval officer drifted across and flopped in a chair alongside.

"What ho, Mac. Why the tears in the beer? Getting ready to shoot yourself?"

"It begins to look like I'm stuck here for life."

"How so?"

"Well, you've been on the *Eagle*, haven't you? She has berthing space for three hundred-odd men, and you need every doggone one of them to operate the darn thing. There isn't a lousy bit of power on the topside. It takes seventy men to hoist a boat the way they've got the gear rigged, and with nothing but fairleads and ring bolts for snatch blocks on deck, it takes about that many men for the necessary hauling, working each mast individually, setting one sail at a time."

"Yep, I think you're pretty much right. She's a brute to handle, and deliberately built so by the Krauts."

"Well, here's my problem, Mr. Anthony. I haven't got more than fifty pairs of willing hands on the whole ship, and now I get word from home that this is all I'm going to get. They made a lot of fine promises last winter, but things are different back there now. They're demobilizing like crazy and haven't got a soul to send over here. It looks like we're going to have to bail out and go home empty-handed."

"How many bodies do you need?"

"I'd love to have two hundred, but I'm willing to gamble with a bare minimum of fifty more."

"Well, old chap, you can have 'em."

I stared at him.

"I *said* you can have 'em, and I *mean* it."

"What are you talking about?"

"I'll lend 'em to you."

"You'll lend me who?"

"Germans, man, Germans—some of the best. I've got tons of 'em."

Seeing the disbelief in my eyes, he went on to say:

"I'm in charge of mine sweeping. I have over a thousand of the buggers working for me. You just take the number you need and I'll keep 'em on my payroll all the time they're gone. When you get to America just dump 'em in a P.O.W. camp and they'll find their way back to me. Mind you, these are not prisoners. They're all ex-navy volunteers. For that matter, why don't you take those boys you have on the *Horst Wessel,* if you like 'em? Tell their captain to come see me tomorrow and I'll sign 'em on as mine swipes. They'll have to be cleared by naval intelligence, if they haven't been already."

It has never been clear how I got away with such an extraordinary bit of business, nor could I figure out how

96

At this moment the *Eagle* is born.

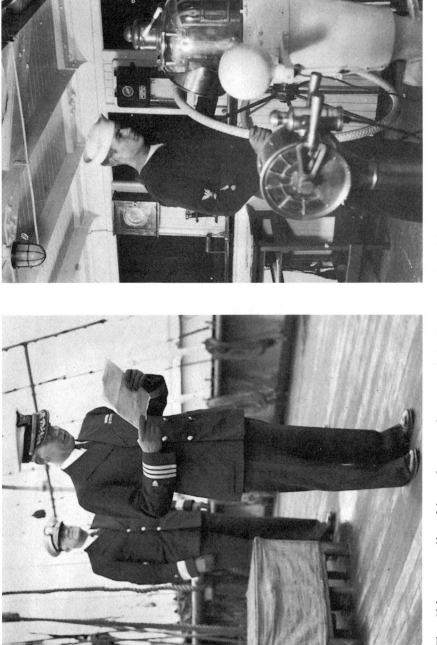

The Skipper reading his orders at the commissioning ceremony.

The Skipper at the age of 19 enlisted in the Coast Guard.

my British friend pulled off his part of the deal without being court-martialed. Whoever learned of this arrangement must have seen it as a simple solution to a complicated problem.

I was so pleased over this stroke of good fortune that I plumb forgot about hurricanes.

Up 'til now the American crew had been commuting from the Navy Barracks. In order to move them on board and set up an official mess, the ship must be in commission. After careful calculation of the time needed to load stores, get the galley range in proper shape, and make the sleeping quarters habitable, it was estimated that we could commission her on the 15th of May.

With mounting excitement and increasing activity, the great day was upon us in a flash. Somehow or other we managed to be ready. Our ship had a gleaming coat of snowy white paint, some of it not yet dry. Her masts were glistening with new spar enamel, and the yards were squared with mathematical precision. Stores and water were shifted until she was on an exact even keel. Her masts seemed taller than before.

The Commodore from the U.S. Naval Command arrived. All hands were drawn up at general muster just forward of the mainm'st. Along the starboard side, facing inboard, were the American enlisted men. On the port side stood the German crew. Lined up athwartships were the officers in double rank, the Americans in front and the Germans in the rear. The Commodore, the Navy Chaplain and I took our stand just forward of the mainm'st facing this U-shaped formation. It had been raining most of the morning, but when the Chaplain stepped forward for a short prayer of dedication the sun came out—surely a good omen.

The Commodore read his orders directing me to place the ship in commission, and handed them to me. I read my own orders, and assumed command. With this, we faced aft at hand salute, and to the accompaniment of shrilling pipes, our national ensign was hauled smartly to the gaff. With the making of colors, I directed the executive officer to "set the watch." The watch standers took their stations. Sideboys fell in at the gangway and the Commodore left the ship.

The new captain gave a short talk to his ship's company. The air was charged with emotion. The Americans were launching into a tremendous adventure. To the Germans this was an act of finality. The ship that many of them had looked upon as a home no longer existed. The Coast Guard Cutter *Eagle* was now a vessel of the United States.

As the formation was dismissed, I glanced at the ranks of the Germans. They were standing stiff as ramrods, tears coursing down their cheeks.

My crew hurried to their quarters for a quick change from their Sunday best back to working clothes. I noticed that the men, although industriously going about their jobs, were subdued and thoughtful. There was none of the customary horseplay.

Ka-Leut came over to me and offered his hand in congratulation, and with a forced smile, disappeared into the cabin area. Up to this time he had been living in the cabin. I had been dreading the day when I would have to move him out of the quarters which had been his home for so long. Now that the day had arrived, he had quietly moved to a spare stateroom, leaving the cabin pin-neat awaiting my occupancy.

I looked around for him to thank him for his courtesy, and discovered his newly selected room. His head was on the desk, his arms outstretched. His shoulders were shaking silently. Seeing that he had not noticed my intrusion, I tiptoed quietly away. Allowing a decent interval to pass, I rang for the cabin boy and asked him to take my invitation to Ka-Leut to have coffee with me in the cabin.

The day the ship went in commission the German crew was put on American rations. This was a tremendous change in diet. After the first meal under the new routine, Von came to the cabin in alarm:

"Cap'n, our commissary hold's not big enough to feed this gang all the way across the Atlantic. They ate up three days' food supply at one meal. They made tall mountains of mashed potatoes on their plates and put about a pint of gravy in the craters at the top, and what they did to the meat you wouldn't believe!"

I soothed Von and decided to await developments. That night Ka-Leut came to the cabin:

"Cap-tain, my crew is all very sick. The change of rations was too rich. The doctor says they will be all right in a little while." Ka-Leut's face was greenish.

"You don't look well yourself, Ka-Leut."

With a sheepish look, and mumbling apologies, he bolted from the cabin.

The next day the German half of the crew was incapacitated. In the days following, they were a sad sight. Their faces broke out in pimples. They developed rashes. Their food consumption per man dropped below the American average. Von's fears were allayed.

The new sails were not finished. The day before our departure from Bremerhaven the last one was taken from the sailmaker's loft, only partially completed. A German bosun's mate with sailmaking experience was taken on, and it was his task to finish the sails during the trip. Working all alone, making each stitch by hand, he barely managed to complete the job on time.

When the first new sails were delivered from Hamburg, excitement ran high as they were hoisted aloft and bent on. They were well made and needed no alteration. We then unbent and sent them below, where they would be neatly rolled and stowed in the sail locker. This bending and unbending of sails was good experience for the green hands. The old sails would be plenty good for the passage down through the English Channel and across the Bay of Biscay. In our inept beginnings, there would be no chance taking of blowing out spanking new sails. We would cut our teeth on expendable stuff.

With the shrouds and stays newly tarred, the masts, yards and gaffs freshly painted, and the running rigging shining with new Manila, the *Eagle* was beginning to look like a ship. After check and double check in every department, I set the sailing date as the 30th of May.

The orders I received for the trip home were unique. I could have obeyed them to the letter and gone home by way of the Suez Canal, India, Thailand, and on through the Panama Canal, taking a year or two to make the trip. They read something like this:

"YOU ARE HEREBY GRANTED THE WIDEST POSSIBLE DISCRE-
TION AS TO THE TIME OF DEPARTURE, ROUTE TO BE
TAKEN, AND PORTS OF CALL AND TIME OF ARRIVAL IN
THE UNITED STATES."

Considering the unusual nature of this mission, however, it would have been unreasonable for them to be worded differently.

After poring over pilot charts, sailing instructions, and all the other publications we could get our hands on, I chose a route which was least likely to get us into trouble. In general, this route runs a close parallel to the first voyage of Columbus. After making passage down the Channel, I proposed to make a departure from the southern tip of England, and slanting southwestward, Funchal, Madeira, would be our first port of call. From Madeira we would continue in the same general direction, picking up the northeast trade winds, and call next at the Canary Islands.

102

From there we would head almost due west on the long haul to St. Thomas, Virgin Islands. We then expected to visit Miami and Bermuda; thence to New London.

That was the original plan. In face of the lateness of our sailing, a new plan was drawn up following the same general route, omitting the calls at the Canary Islands, St. Thomas and Miami.

We were hard pressed to meet our sailing date. There were last minute adjustments of machinery; extra spare parts had to be procured; the water tank, which had given trouble in the ballast episode, had to have a chlorination before it could be pronounced acceptable by the port medical officer.

We had an interesting cargo. In one of the cadet mess rooms trunks, footlockers, a crate of the ship's spare parts, bicycles, and heaven knows what-all was stored. Everything had to be lashed down. There were two mahogany dinghies suspended from the overhead. In addition to this miscellany, there were presents for the Coast Guard Academy. A British naval officer sent a large flag said to have been the personal mark of rank of Grand Admiral Doenitz. There were some fine Plath sextants presented by another ranking officer. If only the weather would hold good for the first few days of the trip! We needed time to make everything secure.

Practically everyone in the Army, Navy and Air Force schemed and plotted to make the trip. Two naval reserve officers who were returning to inactive duty arranged for permission to go. One was a friend of the wardroom officers, and the other was Ted—he of the sour visage—my first apartment mate. A Navy commander (dentist) was on board, and I was happy to have him, not only on the basis of our friendship, but also because he might make himself useful. Our final passenger list included three U.S. naval officers and one Danish officer, the soft spoken former ex-

103

ecutive officer of the *Danmark*. I had seen him in Copenhagen and invited him to come along as my guest, since he wanted to become an American citizen. This would save him the cost of the passage, and it would be a comfort to me to have on board a man of his background.

There were dachshund puppies, wirehaired puppies, and perhaps other pets which may have escaped attention. The tons of souvenirs were mostly worthless and have, no doubt, long since been discarded by their once proud owners. I had visions of encounters with U.S. customs officers, and gave my crew a stern warning that everything, yes *everything* would have to be declared; and that no skulduggery would be tolerated. So far as I could tell, nothing of an unlawful nature came on board.

Among the souvenirs, my prize possession was a delicate piece of Meisen ware I had picked up in Copenhagen—a figurine of a ballet dancer wearing an old fashioned dress of filmy white porcelain lace. I had fallen in love with her on sight and spent my last cent on the purchase.

One night a British major in the Royal Engineers dropped by my quarters for a drink. He spotted Suzie (my name for the figurine), and determined to get her away from me. His first offer was whatever I had paid, which was $34.00. I refused the offer. He would not take no for an answer, and spent the evening upping his price. With each new highball his bid rose. Along about midnight his price hit $600.00. As his determination increased, mine kept pace. Suzie became a cause celebre. The story got out, and I took the ribbing of my life for lavishing so much affection on a piece of porcelain in the middle of the candy bar circuit.

On the day we went in commission I said my goodbyes on Frulingstrasse. My parting from Ducky was on a "See you on Long Island Sound" basis. When I diffidently informed Anna that I was moving to the ship and that very shortly I would be sailing away, I expected some indication of regret at this parting. Ducky and I had been kind to her; we had shared our rations with her, and she had performed her duties cheerfully and well. I thought perhaps she had developed a feeling of attachment for me, as I had for her.

Our parting was as light hearted and offhand as if we were casual acquaintances who had stopped in the street for a bit of gossip. With a quick little nod and a cheery "Auf weidesehen!" I was dismissed, thoroughly deflated.

From the 15th to the 30th of May the weather was uniformly good. All hands agreed that it was sufficiently important to get the ship ready for sailing to justify working seven days a week. As a reward, I promised the men a maximum of privileges in our ports of call. Their true reward lay in the satisfaction derived from bringing the *Eagle* to life.

On sailing day we were a cocky lot.

Chapter VII

On May 29th we left our mooring and spent most of the day swinging ship for compass compensation in the Weser River estuary.

Although all modern ships carry gyro compasses, the good old magnetic compass is basic equipment, and is carefully maintained by all prudent navigators. The gyro indicates true north, and saves time and labor in laying down courses. It is a steady compass and easy to steer by, but gyro compasses have been known to fail through a mechanical disorder or failure of the ship's current. A careless navigator who has ignored his magnetic compass for any length of time is immediately lost when his gyro fails. Although the magnetic compass, in theory, points toward the magnetic pole, in actual practice, due to a tendency of the steel structure in a ship to pick up stray magnetism, it nearly always has minor errors which should be known to the navigator in order that he may apply the necessary corrections to his courses.

Swinging a ship for compass compensation is a fairly simple procedure. The ship is taken to quiet waters where there is enough room to maneuver. The navigator, or the commercial compass expert, heads the ship true north, then swings to south, and east and west, each time jotting down on a work sheet the difference between the true heading and the magnetic compass heading. From these observations he then determines how well or how badly his compass is behaving, and is able to counteract abnormal magnetic influences around the compass by placing small permanent magnets below or near the compass, which, by his calculations, cancel the magnetic disturbances within the ship that cause the misbehavior.

After he has corrected as well as he can, the ship is then headed north once more and swung slowly in a large circle, stopping long enough every fifteen degrees to take a quiet, steady reading on those headings. This last maneuver is called "swinging for residuals." The residual errors—magnetic remnants that it is not worth while to further correct, are entered in columns opposite the various fifteen degree headings. This card becomes the deviation table and is mounted under glass near the magnetic compass, where the navigator can, at a glance, pick off the corrections he needs for the course which he may be laying down on a chart.

Due to the interruptions of passing traffic, swinging ship usually takes most of a day.

After ship compensation was completed we anchored. A gentle drizzling rain set in about sunset. Last minute loading went on through most of the night.

About eleven o'clock I took a turn around the deck to see how the loading was going. A boat was alongside and stores were being hoisted on board by means of a small davit forward of the gangway. My attention fastened to a row of rather large crates which bore the stenciled legend "Typewriters." Knowing we were short on typewriters, I had a closer look. One of the boxes was big enough to contain a piano. It also had a stenciled legend: "Ship collect to Col. Whosis," and gave an address somewhere in Virginia. I hailed the Exec:

"Whose stuff is this?"

"I don't know, Cap'n. I thought it was some friend of yours."

"Well, I never heard of this Colonel Whosis. Ask the other officers."

Nobody knew the colonel in question.

"How much of this stuff is aboard, and where did it come from?"

"There are eleven boxes, Cap'n, lined up right here in front of us, and that is all. An army truck backed up on the pier and the men laid the stuff down alongside our stores and one of them said: 'This stuff is for the *Eagle*'."

Pointing to another crate:

"That box there is the exact same size as a fifty bottle case of cognac. Lord knows what is in some of the others."

Shortly before this, there had been stories in the press about attempts on the part of a few members of the armed forces to sneak home art treasures and other loot. It was possible that this extraordinary attempt at shipment might not cover criminal activity, but there was obviously something sneaky going on.

"Take the stuff back and dump it on the pier where you got it."

"The pier is deserted and unguarded now, Cap'n. The Germans will probably loot that stuff before morning."

"That's no skin off my back. It's my guess that the stuff was looted in the first place. Anyway, the rain is going to give it a good soaking before morning."

It's possible that I may have met Colonel Whosis somewhere, but this unannounced night delivery was, to say the least, presumptuous. As it was, a lot of the cargo was extraordinary in nature and was going to require rather more than a cursory examination on the part of the customs people. At least, I knew the true nature of everything stashed around the ship now and intended to be absolutely candid with the customs inspectors. An unknown colonel was certainly not going to get a privilege I had denied to my own ship's company. Besides, if they really were typewriters, what the hell was he doing with so many?

Dawn came bright and clear, but with a dead calm. I put on a show of being disappointed at not having any

108

breeze, but the cold truth is I had more than a little bit of a feeling of relief. We would sail under power. The people on the beach would not get a chance to criticize any clumsiness on our part. There was certain to be awkwardness and fumbling in our first setting of sails under way. The crew grumbled about not having any breeze, but in their secret hearts, I suspect they felt the same relief. Under power alone and in the absence of a head wind, we could make ten knots—a surprising speed for a 1700-ton ship with such a small amount of horsepower, but understandable when you consider the smooth lines of her underwater body. Of course, in a head breeze this speed is knocked off sharply.

Under the regulations, a channel pilot was required for all ships because of the many miles of mine-infested water which must be skirted. Scotty had previously agreed to act as my pilot as far as Falmouth, since he wanted to visit his family. He had the necessary license, and I was delighted to have him as a guest.

It is 700 miles from Bremerhaven to Falmouth by the route we had to take. This seemed a very long time for the ship to be under pilotage, but I remembered a case that could top it.

When the Coast Guard had three cutters built at Point Pleasant, West Virginia, in the 1930's, I made the trip from there to New Orleans as an observer. On that occasion we carried pilots for 1900 miles. At the time the ships were still in the custody of the builders, and I was free as a bird to sightsee and live a fat cat existence. How different things were now. Scotty's presence was simply to furnish technical assistance. The responsibility was all mine.

For use in fog or in giving passing signals when she is operating under power, the *Eagle* has a magnificent air horn, mounted high upon the mainm'st. Every vessel in the harbor bade farewell to us with three long blasts on the whistle. Our answering blasts were deep-toned and musical.

Because the ship was anchored in fairly shallow water, our hand-powered windlass got only a brief workout as we weighed anchor. Von's best efforts to scrounge a power windlass for the anchor had been fruitless. He had visited a number of shipyards and had found many winches. All he unearthed were either mighty monsters designed to handle cargo on big freighters, or little pipsqueak yacht winches. Thus, part of our role as fundamental seafarers was thrust upon us.

The boys at the capstan bars were just getting warmed up when the signal came—"Anchor's aweigh!" Assisted by a moderate ebb tide, we squared off down the channel with our diesel exhaust barely audible. Toward the outer harbor limits the clear atmosphere gave way to haze, and in a short time we lost sight of the watchers on the beach.

Getting from Bremerhaven to Falmouth was a complicated piece of business. Leaving the Weser River estuary, the course crossed an arm of the North Sea just below Helgoland and followed a swept channel down through the Strait of Dover, rounding the Thames estuary, past Southampton and into Falmouth.

The swept channel was one mile wide, with an additional mile on either side marked "swept but doubtful." This area had been showered with mines during the war and was extremely hazardous. As a precaution against bad weather which might blow us off our precarious course, we took a German tug as an escort. The degaussing system had to be in operation until we passed Southampton, where the water was sufficiently deep to eliminate the danger of magnetic mines. The whole area was cluttered with skeletons of sunken ships. Here and there a mast protruded from the water. A narrow channel threaded its way among these reminders of disaster.

110

Eddie Didion and the dachshunds.

Eddie lines up with the liberty party.

There was a harbor pilot on board the *Eagle* for the first few miles. When the pilot boat came alongside to take him off, I performed a painful duty.

Early in the fitting out period, a handsome youngster with blond curly hair, had been hanging around the gangway. He appeared to be about ten years old, and, in contrast to most German children, was rosy-cheeked and looked well fed. One day he showed up on deck in a miniature suit of dungarees, wielding a paint brush alongside one of my men.

He spoke English with no trace of an accent. On being questioned he told the following story: His name was Eddie Didion. He was born somewhere in France, near Normandy, and had become orphaned in the early days of the war. When Normandy was invaded by the Allies, Eddie attached himself to an American regiment and had been unofficially adopted. After nearly two years with what he called his "old outfit," the regiment had sailed for home from Bremerhaven. He had tried to stow away for that trip but had been caught and put off the ship. He followed the waterfront until he came to the *Eagle,* and joined my crew.

His training in the army had been excellent. He always said "Sir" when spoken to; he stood at attention when addressed; he kept himself neat and clean and had a warm and friendly smile for everyone. It was easy to understand how the ingratiating little devil had wormed his way into the affections of the men. At this time the crew seriously wanted to adopt him. One of my men nominated himself as a would-be foster parent, but was told by the Red Cross that the boy's doubtful origin would make it nearly impossible.

Eddie's status as a crew member became more firmly established each day. He acquired a hammock, a suit of blues; he even had his own deck scrubber. One evening as I watched a liberty inspection from the quarterdeck, I

113

spotted Eddie in the ranks. He was immaculate, his little shoes sparkling from a last minute buffing. His mop of curls had been dampened and combed back to permit the proper rakish slant to his flat hat. The officer of the deck received a smart salute from Eddie. He halted at the head of the gangway, faced aft and saluted the colors, faced left again and marched proudly ashore. As he and his friends sauntered down the wharf toward the recreation center, I noticed a distinct nautical roll in his gait.

On sailing day Eddie was nowhere in sight, nor had he been in evidence the day before. To all appearances he had deserted us. I knew better. A search of the ship *before* we sailed would have been useless. I called the crew together and told all hands that Eddie must be produced forthwith. No Eddie—no sail.

They looked stunned. What a revolting development! Their faces showed plainly that they had hoped to "discover" the stowaway after the ship was well out at sea and committed to the crossing.

It took about half an hour, but they dragged him, kicking and biting, to the ship's side. Reproachful looks were aimed in my direction as they lowered him gently over the side. The pilot boat swung away, Eddie a tiny bit of human misery in the cockpit. His heartbroken weeping continued as he dropped astern. He never looked back.

I regretted the whole episode, and mentally kicked myself for letting this attachment develop. I had already told the Red Cross to expect Eddie back on the pilot boat, and knew he would be taken care of.

The first day at sea was crowded with activity. The fact that there was no breeze was of little consequence since sailing maneuvers in these restricted waters would have been dangerous business. Our channel was marked at the turning points by light ships, with widely spaced buoys at

114

intervals between. If the weather should hold as it was now, this part of the trip would be uneventful.

Now for some housekeeping. Hoses were led out on the topside and the air was filled with sounds of the swishing deck scrubbers and sloshing water as we began the task of removing the accumulated grime of our days in port from the fine teak decks. Seamen armed with buckets and hand swabs went to work on the paint and bright work. The fancy business of shining brass could wait until we got into the balmy weather of the trade winds. While part of the crew was engaged on the topside, still more were trying to bring order out of the chaos of our hasty loading down below. An occasional yelp from one of the puppies underfoot testified to the industry below decks.

Lashing down loose gear as the ship puts to sea is a good precaution and should never be neglected, but in spite of everyone's best efforts, some things are overlooked on every sailing day. When the vessel begins to roll and pitch, unsecured gear makes its own announcement.

All day we chugged along on a smooth sea. The haze limited visibility, but we were still able to see the channel markers. Milky vapor rose from water to sky, blotting out the horizon, giving the illusion that the ship sat in the middle of an enormous shallow saucer. Only evidence of progress was the V of our wake and the occasional passing of buoys. We appeared to hold our position in space under a vacant sky, while the earth rolled beneath us.

The washing down and the hum of activity below decks were sounds of unity. We were a tight little community, busily putting our house in order. To the right Helgoland passed, silent and mysterious, invisible in the murk. To the left the north German coast and the Netherlands slid past unnoted as the navigator identified each buoy on the chart, tracking our progress with neat, precise notations of the times each was passed and the distance abeam.

Single and double taps on the ship's bell ticked off the passage of the half hours. As the magic figure of eight was reached, a watch was completed. The cycle would begin again with a single stroke marking the end of the first half hour of the new watch.

I remained constantly on the quarterdeck. Not a precious moment was I willing to waste below decks while our vessel was being reborn. A ship at anchor or shackled to a pier goes downhill. Every day spent in port subtly eats at her vitals. Every day at sea sharpens the skill of the ship's company and adds to the feeling that a ship really lives and has personality, be it good or bad. This Teutonic emigrant still bore signs of her old self, but everywhere there was change. Among ships there are bums that go from one misadventure to another throughout their lives, sometimes fetching up on rocks or shoals as a fitting climax to a misspent life. The *Eagle* came from good stock and had led a well-ordered life. Her new company was determined to keep her record unblemished.

Our tug had sailed ahead of us and we overtook her in mid-afternoon. She was directed to keep us in sight in case she was needed.

An hour before sunset a gentle breeze came up from dead ahead. Although the breeze swept the haze away and brought out a knife-edged horizon, the zephyr was worse than useless. It slowed us down. When we rounded the point where the course was changed to enter the upper approaches of the English Channel, the breeze hauled, and was from dead ahead.

As we squared away on our new course, the breeze became brisk. During the next hour our speed was cut in half. As the hours went by and the breeze freshened, movement ahead fell off to a crawl. We blinked across to the tug and signalled for a tow line. She hove up under the bowsprit and tossed us a line.

116

All the second day the wind continued from directly ahead. With our expanse of rigging and yards aloft acting as a brake, we would have gotten nowhere without assistance from the tug.

As the wind veered off to port or starboard, there came times when the setting of a few stays'ls might assist the ship's progress. This was tried, but the wind was never far enough off of dead ahead for the sails to draw. We were impatient to put on sail, but I was forced to abandon the idea until the weather changed. As we moved southward, the weather got steadily worse.

On the third day the sky clouded over and a cold misty rain set in. The chill penetrated to our bones. Watches consisted of a monotonous round of checking bearings on the occasional light houses and beacons which went dragging by. We had not planned for this wintry stuff. There had been no intention of using the heating system and it was not in commission. Thanks to Von's foresight, there was a supply of blankets on board, and they came out of their wrappings.

The southerly wind squeezing through the Strait of Dover picked up speed and held us back. We seemed to take hours to pass a given point. Opposite the Thames estuary the going was tricky. Here lay the biggest concentration of sunken hulls. In these waters the magnetic mine had paid off for the Germans before counter measures could be devised. It was a piece of good luck that the breeze began to fall off and our slight increase in speed made the tow more manageable and our navigation more precise.

I devoutly hoped that the degaussing and deperming job the engineers had performed before we left Bremerhaven would protect us. It was almost a certainty that we were steaming over a few of those deadly gadgets buried in the mud beyond the reach of the diligent mine sweepers. As we neared the area off Southampton where the bottom drops

117

off and deep water offers a measure of safety, I kept an eagle eye on the depth recorder. When the needle showed a depth of 100 feet with a rapid increase, I heaved a sigh of relief.

"Secure the degaussing system."

At the end of the fourth day, when we rounded the point of land just outside Falmouth harbor entrance, we cast off the hawser. Unless he is raised on barges, a sailor instinctively hates the idea of being dragged along behind a tug. If there is any towing to be done, he'd rather do it himself.

As the harbor pilot boarded us, his manner bespoke keen interest in this out-of-the-ordinary craft. We dropped anchor in the quiet harbor with something of a feeling of anti-climax. The passage had been dull and monotonous. It had been uncomfortable and cold.

The *Eagle* drew crowds to the waterfront, and was promptly surrounded by small boats. The crew developed a tendency to swagger in the manner of old salts under the eyes of the admiring crowds.

When I paid my call on the senior British naval officer present, he invited me to bring my Exec to dinner the following night. As we drove to his home a few miles out of town the next afternoon, I saw the glorious green countryside of England for the first time. The ancient road reminded me of the Old Trace near Natchez, Mississippi. The velvety fields with stone fences had the air of being unchanged for centuries. The commander lived in a gray stone house completely overgrown with ivy, in keeping with the surrounding countryside. His wife gave us a warm welcome. A large log crackled in the fireplace, and we were grateful for the warmth. The countryside was feeling the chill of the storm which was raging offshore.

Our hostess was modestly proud of the meal. Obviously, this was better than their average daily fare. It was simple and bore authentic marks of austerity. The main course

118

was a meat loaf with a "long splice" of oatmeal. To show my appreciation of their hospitality, I invited the commander and his wife to come on board the *Eagle* for dinner the following evening. Scotty and his wife, who had met us in Falmouth, completed the party. There was bad weather continuing offshore and this held us in port.

Everyone was in good spirits and I was enjoying my first cabin party. All went well until the cabin boy started to bring in the food. The steward, bursting with pride at this premiere performance, had outdone himself. Enormous steaks, dripping with butter and surrounded by mounds of mushrooms, were piled high on a huge platter—a vulgar display of wealth.

I was scarlet with embarrassment, but attempted to keep the conversation rolling. The guests apparently failed to notice, and showed obvious enjoyment of the meal. I concealed a sigh of relief—too early in the game. Immediately after coffee, my party fell apart. Offering hasty excuses, the guests departed.

Our rich food was having the same effect that it had had on the German sailors. In this respect World War II affected victors and vanquished alike.

Chapter VIII

It had been my intention to remain in Falmouth only long enough to take fuel and stores. A storm of considerable size was sweeping the outer coast of England, so we discreetly stayed in port until it had passed. On the fourth morning the blow had abated.

At the end of the first week in June we took our departure from Land's End. The storm had blown by and left calm weather in its wake. As we cleared the headland of Falmouth entrance, we began to feel the Atlantic swell. Here at last was the real beginning of our voyage.

In the old days a sailing ship having departed with the tide, would have slatted about waiting for the first breeze before the journey could be started. Time would not permit this bit of authenticity. The engine was kept going all day. Having no steadying effect from sails, we wallowed around in the swells as Land's End became a faint line, and slowly dropped down over the horizon.

Our rolling dislodged everything that had not been properly secured. Throughout the ship came the clattering and banging of loose gear. The aftermath of bad weather is a long smooth swell, slow in subsiding. This deep breathing of the ocean imparts motion to a ship which betrays a sloppy seaman. I smiled to myself as the sounds gradually subsided. How many times had I heard the same thing on destroyers, cutters and patrol boats! I could predict almost to the minute the length of time it would take to quiet the ship down.

When the ship made its first noticeable roll, a noise like a pistol shot rang out amidships. I leaped to the forward railing of the quarterdeck in time to see the bosun's mate picking up a four-inch shackle from the top of the engine room hatch. It had narrowly missed a man's head on its downward plunge! At some time during the fitting out period one of the crew had negligently laid it on a flat surface somewhere aloft and forgotten it. This lethal gadget had been hanging over our heads ever since we left Bremerhaven!

With an anxious eye I searched the rigging. One of our safety rules had been that nothing should be carried aloft without being secured on a lanyard. This narrow escape was proof that our accident-free record included a generous helping of luck.

All day I was plagued with a premonition of impending disaster. Faith in our ability to negotiate the next 5000 miles melted away. The falling shackle seemed a bad omen. This pessimism is nothing new. It is the only form of sea-sickness I have ever known. Throughout my career I have been plagued with the first-day-at-sea-blues.

In planning the trip I had regarded the Bay of Biscay as the most dangerous part of the passage. On pilot charts and sailing instructions it is plainly indicated that the weather here is unpredictable and capricious. The bold coast lines of France, Spain and Portugal offer few refuges in case a ship is forced to seek shelter. In the days of sail many ships had been wrecked here. Perhaps I was worrying needlessly, but I wanted all odds in our favor, especially on this part of the trip. As a result, the engine was kept chugging along at standard speed, and no particular effort was made to whistle up a breeze.

For generations, whistling on board ship, for a very practical reason, has carried the taint of superstition. Young seamen were told by their oldsters that whistling on board ship is bad luck and is certain to bring on a storm. The purpose of this installed superstition was to discourage any sound that would compete with the bosun's pipe. The old timers could pass along almost every necessary nautical command through use of the language of the pipe. A variation of the superstition is that if you whistle softly, you will get a nice fresh breeze, but maybe from the wrong direction. I was just superstitious enough to not tempt fate.

The second day I was up and about as the navigator was completing work on his star sights. As I sipped at a mug of coffee still too hot to drink, I watched the stars fade. The coming of day on a clear, calm morning is a quiet, still thing. To the east the deep blue gently fades to pale violet, and gives way to delicate rosy opalescence. Across the sky from north to south a giant curtain sweeps silently westward, unveiling the new day. The horizon sharpens as the golden glow from the still hidden sun erases the black stain of night from the surface of the water. The only breeze was from ahead, created by our motion through the still air.

The executive officer pointed to a tiny triangle he had placed on our course line well ahead of our estimated morning position.

"We've got a fair current, Cap'n. Must have been carrying it all night. We're gaining on Madeira even without wind. Sure would like to get some canvas on."

"That position is a little too good to be true. You wouldn't fake for the Old Man's benefit, would you?"

"Oh, no, Cap'n. This is one of the best mornings I have seen for sights. She's steady as a church this morning and I had a needle sharp horizon. We know within a few hundred yards exactly where we are."

"Well, let's hope for some breeze."

I went below for some breakfast.

Some time later an excited messenger rapped on the cabin door.

"Cap'n, the OD says we got a breeze coming up."

122

"Lay aloft, lay out and unfurl!"

German sailors squaring a yard at the capstan.

I hurried to the quarterdeck. In the path of the morning sun ripples were furrowing the surface of the water. The breeze was coming in from the port quarter—exactly what we wanted. I watched a moment as it freshened. I glanced at the Exec, and saw from his eager expression that he was anxious for some action. I gave him a nod. He picked up a megaphone:

"All hands fall in at quarters!"

The crew scrambled to their stations.

"Lay aloft, lay out and unfurl!"

The men raced up the ratlines to their sail stations. The passengers assembled on the after area of the quarterdeck to share in this thrilling moment. In feverish excitement the sailors bellied over the yards and began unfastening the gaskets. In a light breeze and to celebrate this special occasion, we were unfurling man-o-war style, which means that the sails should appear at one command as if by magic. This is best performed with a full complement, and our skeletonized crew could only approximate such an operation. Under normal conditions, in the future we would set the sails one by one.

After the unfurling and when the sails were ready for setting, the men in the rigging secured the loose ends of the gaskets and came swarming down on deck, where the real fun began. In putting sail on, an attempt is made to keep the ship balanced. Here the word "balance" means equalizing of the tendency of the vessel to carry lee or weather helm. If the bow falls off before the wind under a heads'l, then the rudder will have to be put over correspondingly to equalize this. However, by putting more sail on aft, the same result can be obtained, and the tendency to go right or left can be made to balance by the symmetrical arrangement of the sails.

Setting sail on a square-rigger can be in almost any order that suits the purposes of the skipper. If setting sail is a

125

part of maneuvering the vessel in confined waters, the order in which the sails should be set becomes demanding of a high degree of skill. In the open sea, with an auxiliary engine, there is nothing to do but place the ship at the desired angle to the breeze and go on about the business of piling on canvas.

With the wind abaft the beam—and ours was practically from astern—we first set what are called the lower courses; that is, the fores'l and mains'l—the two lowest and largest sails. After some order was restored to the snarled-up lines on deck, the tops'ls were set.

The *Eagle* carries double tops'ls. The lower tops'ls sheet to the fore and main yards, and the upper tops'ls sheet to the lower tops'l yards. Large full-rigged ships frequently carried double to'gallants'ls, but the *Eagle's* was single, which meant that a larger individual sail was carried, but under a simpler sheeting and bracing arrangement, since there was one less yard to contend with on each mast.

By the time we got the courses and tops'ls set, we turned our attention to the fo'castle and quarterdeck. We first set the foretopm'st stays'l, and I watched the lubber's line at the steering stand, ordering the helmsman to hold the wheel amidships. By this time we had come around and had the wind two points abaft the beam on the port tack. The bow started falling off to starboard. Without correcting this error in heading, we ran out the lower mizzens'l and the *Eagle,* like a perfect lady, curtseyed, and turned obediently to port. This was almost an exactly even balance between the foretopm'st stays'l and the lower mizzens'l.

Had the breeze been stiffer, our first venture in sailing would have been limited to the sails just described. The breeze steadied at about force three or four, and, gaining confidence and courage, we put everything on.

With her sails beginning to draw, the *Eagle* was a beauti-

126

ful thing. First inkling of bad news came when I witnessed the wild behavior of the main tacks and sheets. In a twinkling, the parallel purchases of the tackles twisted and writhed like a family of snakes. The blocks on the hauling end spiralled until further movement in the direction of the lay of the line was impossible. The main sheets and tacks were of five-inch line—the new Manila we had so proudly appropriated in Bremerhaven. Aloft, all the line we had been renewing in the past weeks was easy to spot. It was busily knotting itself into rats' nests as though it had a will of its own.

Shortening down to tops'ls, lower courses, the fore topm'st stays'l and lower mizzen, we began the drudgery of putting our house in order.

By sunset we furled everything but the lower courses and lower tops'ls. This was a safety precaution. I was not about to let green seamen scramble to sail stations in the darkness until they were completely familiar with every line to be encountered on the way up and on the way down. For this reason we stuck to the strongest and safest sails during the night, feeling that an unexpected squall could do little harm with all the tall stuff put away. This limitation remained in force all the way to Madeira.

The first night under sail alone I meticulously specified the sails to be carried during the night watches, emphasizing the fact that no sail could be set without my permission, but that sail could be taken off at the discretion of the officer of the deck, in which case the commanding officer should be immediately notified.

Toward midnight I alternated between pacing back and forth along the port side of the quarterdeck and resting occasionally in one of the deck chairs we had roused from the hold that morning. It has long been a custom of mine to mentally rehearse emergencies at sea, trying to predict my probable reactions. I had been taught by one of my

127

early skippers to go over these imaginary drills each time I took a watch at sea.

I would go over the procedure which I most likely would follow if I suddenly received word that a man had fallen overboard—say on the starboard side aft. In operating a vessel under power I would know the answer, having gone through this many times. Obviously, this was an entirely different situation. With the ship on the port tack, a man going over the starboard quarter would have to fight his way away from the side because of the slight leeway we were making. Our travel being at a small angle down wind from our actual heading, we would have a tendency to drag down on the man.

How get the ship back to the spot where the man went over? Assuming that we would have time to drop a light buoy near him, would it be better to come down with all the sails, lower a boat and have the boat row back to him; or would it be saving in time to bring the ship around and sail back toward the spot where the man had gone over? At this stage in my experience I simply did not know the answer. Either maneuver could go wrong in a big way. Best we don't let anybody fall overboard right now.

As I puzzled over an assortment of situations which *might* arise, the seriousness of my position as a green skipper of a green crew came fully into focus for the first time. At this moment I earnestly wished I could turn the ship around and head back for the safety of Falmouth harbor before it was too late.

Suppose a youngster should slip and fall from the royal yard to almost certain death tomorrow morning? This would surely bring a searching investigation, wherein my fitness for the assignment would get a cold, dispassionate going over. The answers would be obvious.

To hell with such thoughts! I was talking myself into a state of defeatism. Come hell or high water, I was com-

128

mitted to a voyage of 4900 miles and the smart thing to do was my level best. Foresight and thoroughness in preparation for emergencies were indispensable now, but there should be no room in my thoughts for apprehensiveness or timidity. I would do my best. Angels could do no better.

I took some comfort from a remark I had heard from an old timer:

"It's not the greenhorns who fall screaming down from aloft. It's the old timers who are so damn sure of themselves they get careless and reach behind them for a line that isn't there."

I had noticed that the youngsters had sticky fingers when aloft. So long as they didn't get *too* sticky, we would be all right. Once or twice on the *Danmark* I had seen men freeze with fear on their first trip up into the rigging. It had been necessary to send bosun's mates up to pry them loose and lower them away to the deck lashed in a bosun's chair. We had found no freezers among the *Eagle's* boys.

There would be little likelihood of meeting another sailing vessel during the trip, and every seaman knows that a vessel under sail has the right of way over all vessels under power unless the sailing ship is overtaking. This was good. All the other ships we encountered would just have to stay out of our way.

Aside from a possible man overboard incident, men raining down from the rigging, potential collisions, perhaps a fire in the paint locker, there was always the intriguing prospect of nasty weather. According to all the accumulated sea lore, the next few days should be watched prayerfully. Once beyond the Bay of Biscay, say down around the latitude of Gibraltar, we could be reasonably sure of pretty summer weather the rest of the way home.

My sleeping quarters were in the "sea cabin," a small room which opens on the quarterdeck. Next morning I was awakened just after dawn by the sound of commands from the quarterdeck, and men moving about on the topside. Remembering the wording of the night orders, I lost no time in getting on deck to see what emergency had dictated the taking in of sails. I was shocked to see men in the act of unfurling and setting new sail, sails that had been forbidden.

When the OD was asked why he was disobeying the orders in the night order book, he showed genuine surprise and embarrassment. He had seen the cabin boy heading aft with coffee and assumed that the captain was up and about, and felt that it would be wise to show a little initiative by setting some sail, it being broad daylight and the weather really fine. He said he knew in advance that I would approve and give automatic permission—he just had not gotten around to sending a messenger down to make the token request.

I assured him that the night orders were binding, and that it would be well not to anticipate the captain's approval in the future. Having made this same mistake as a junior officer, I understood his feelings and let him off more lightly than I had been dealt with under similar circumstances; nevertheless, I made it clear that this was not a trivial matter. It was my mission to get the ship to the States in good shape and within a reasonable time. No detail nor bit of routine was unimportant if it had any bearing on the safety of this half-green crew.

"Half-green," because they were beginning to look like real salty sailormen. The renewal of the lines in the rigging, a mixed blessing, taught the crew line handling and marlinspike seamanship. The bending on of new sails while in Bremerhaven, and then the unbending and stowing away, did its part in the schooling.

On the third day out of Falmouth, "Doc," our navy dentist passenger, came to me with some news. He had become friendly with the German physician Ka-Leut had brought along, and learned from him of the condition of one of the German seamen. This young man had a large open lesion in his side. The wound, which had refused to heal, was a carryover from the war. At the time the Germans were being recruited for the trip, this youngster had managed to conceal his condition. I do not know whether Ka-Leut and the German doctor had foreknowledge, but they appeared innocent in the affair.

Upon questioning, the boy stated that he had concealed the wound hoping that after he got to America he could get treatment and perhaps plastic surgery. He had been treated in German hospitals, with no sign of healing. It came out that his wound was the result of his having been shot down by the Soviets in a Messerschmidt fighter over the Eastern front eighteen months before. He was able to work, and there had been no complaints from his shipmates. Since we were well out at sea—probably the way the boy had planned it—there was nothing to do but ask the doctor to pay close attention to him and do what he could. The boy was only nineteen. At that age I was just entering the service as an apprentice seaman, fresh from the sticks. I could not help but feel sympathy for this young man who was a wounded war veteran at such a tender age.

"Doc" had been engaged in making training films in prosthetics, but was highly skilled in straight dental work. When he came on board, he was informally designated as ship's dentist. One day he and I were taking a breather on the quarterdeck back of the chart house when the report came aft that there was a toothache to be treated. Doc sauntered forward in the general direction of his stateroom, and I gazed at the sky, wondering if the good weather would hold. After what seemed like no more than two minutes, he came drifting back and settled into his deck chair. As he reached for a nearby book, I wanted to know what he was going to do about the toothache.

131

"Oh, I took care of that."

"What did you do?"

"I pulled it."

"Why, man, you didn't have time to use an anesthetic. You must have killed the poor guy!"

"No, I'm no Chinese dentist; I just happen to know how to give novocain."

I sneaked down to the quarters to satisfy my curiosity. The "victim" had not felt a thing. Doc was a lightning operator.

As we got clear of the coast of Europe, Doc casually mentioned the famous appendicitis operation performed by a pharmacist's mate during World War II on a submarine in the Pacific. I caught a gleam in his eye as he drawled:

"You know, I've done nothing but dentistry, but I sort of think I could handle a job like that without all the fuss and feathers. Skipper, we're going to be a long time gone between Madeira and Bermuda. That course you've got there takes us 3000 miles and away from the steamship lanes. What if somebody develops an ailment needing an operation?"

The idea disturbed me, but I refused to make a commitment.

"We'll face that when we get to it."

This got me to thinking. We had a German doctor on board, whose credentials were excellent. Ka-Leut said that his reputation was tops, both as a physician and a surgeon. Just what would I do?

I recalled my qualms about our former enemies when I was on my way to Germany. Could they be trusted? Were they likely to slit our throats as we slept some night once the ship was at sea, and make off for some distant island where they would scuttle the ship and live as forgotten men? All this nonsense had been replaced with a little more realistic view of things, thanks to the experience of the

132

past five months; but just suppose I should develop an appendicitis case in mid-Atlantic—a really hot case that had to be operated on at once? Then, in spite of his skill, the German doctor might operate and the patient die? How would this be received back home? On the other hand, for fear of trusting an enemy, I entrust such a case to friend Doc, and he messes up the job.

Neither prospect was very pleasant, and I hoped I would not be faced with such a dilemma.

Ka-Leut's last official act before the commissioning ceremony was to make me a present of Heinz. He was indentured to my service for as long as the Germans should be on board. As Ka-Leut's cabin boy in Bremerhaven, Heinz had anticipated his commanding officer's every wish. In spite of his stiff military manner, he conveyed the impression of being utterly devoted and solicitous. He was about five feet two, of stocky build, with a mop of ashy blond hair combed straight back over his ears in the style currently popular among German youth. He rarely smiled, seeming to have no time for frivolous nonsense. When spoken to, he wore the intent look so common among the hard-of-hearing. Whenever Ka-Leut addressed his remarks to Heinz, he always spoke in a soft voice, so it was obvious that Heinz's hearing was good; his features were merely expressing his attitude. He stood at attention with every muscle.

On most ships the skipper is pretty much a night owl. I was no exception. On the *Eagle* I usually retired anywhere between two A.M. and dawn, and would sleep an hour or two in the morning or afternoon. No matter how irregular my hours, Heinz's sixth sense told him within minutes the time I would awaken. The first few mornings I woke up to find him entering the cabin with hot coffee, I attributed his promptness to luck. After a week, I was convinced that he discreetly peeped until he got the first signs of the beginning of my coming to life, and timed his entry to coincide with my becoming consciously awake. If this was his method, he was a fast worker. On the whole trip across, in port as well as at sea, Heinz never missed.

When Ka-Leut gave him to me, it did not seem possible that he would be able to transfer such dedicated zeal from one officer to another while remaining on the same ship, but this seemed to be no problem to Heinz. I could detect not the slightest change in his attitude as he entered into my service. He knew only a little English, but did not appear to need language in his unerring ability to anticipate the wants of his boss. For once in my life, I had the pleasant experience of having at my beck and call a perfect servant.

In addition to Heinz, there were three or four young German stewards on board. One thing they shared in common—they had raised flowing manes of hair four to six inches in length, combed straight back almost to the napes of their necks. This practice was widespread in Germany, in fact, had been taken up in Scandinavia. I was told that the Danes bullied their young boys into cutting their dank locks by accusing them of trying to look like Germans.

The first day out I asked Ka-Leut to call these youngsters in and tell them that, as food handlers, they would have to get haircuts. The reaction was surprising. They protested vehemently. Ka-Leut, with some embarrassment, directed two of his huskiest older boys to drag these rebels to the barbershop and see that they were properly shorn. When they returned on deck, two of them were weeping, and Heinz slunk into the cabin, his head hanging in shame.

I asked Heinz directly why they had so strongly objected to getting a haircut. After fumbling for an answer, he blurted out:

"We have lost our manhood."

The Americans wondered about this mysterious behavior, and could only speculate as to its cause. In the light

134

of Heinz's explanation, we thought perhaps Germany's defeat had left the future outlook so bleak for German youth that the growing of a head of long hair, although just a fad, took on special symbolism.

Our broken-hearted boys recovered quickly. In a few days they were wearing their crew cuts proudly.

Chapter IX

From Land's End to Madeira is 1400 nautical miles. The early stages of this leg of the trip were filled with anxiety over the chance that sudden bad weather might catch us while we were still so vulnerable. Every waking hour and all of our energy were devoted to the job at hand. The breeze subsided from time to time, making it necessary to resume the use of power, but I was not too proud to start up the engine in order to get us below the latitude of Gibraltar.

The days were successively better ordered and more smoothly organized. I blessed the good weather while we were fighting to get the kinks out of our snarled up lines. The job was not easily accomplished because of our short-handed condition.

In the early days in Bremerhaven I had shuddered at the sight of so much bronze and steel in the upper rigging. We had wire rope braces, steel topmasts and steel yards. The gear aloft was awfully heavy and hard on the hands, but the wire rope never snarled up nor became balky.

After the incident of the first setting of sails, we were slow in getting back to the point of putting them all on again. About the fourth or fifth day out, we achieved some semblance of order aloft and got around to setting the to'ga'ns'ls and royals. On the mizzenm'st the *Eagle* had a double gaff, which permitted the setting of three separate sails—the lower mizzen, the upper mizzen and the mizzen tops'l. With the mizzens'ls divided thus, it was not necessary to reef the lower mizzen on account of its small size. The double gaff arrangement has been criticized by some of

136

Double mizzen with mizzen topsail set.

the few remaining square-riggermen alive, and referred to as typically Teutonic. Later in the voyage I was to have occasion to bless the Teutonic designers responsible for this rig.

Balancing the mizzenm'st sail arrangement is one of the prettiest groupings of sails to be found on ships. Starting at the bow and moving out along the bowsprit, we come successively to four triangular sails with romantic names. I have already referred to the foretopm'st stays'l as balancing the lower mizzens'l. The other three are the inner jib, the outer jib and the flying jib. To complete the picture stays'ls named after the stay to which they are attached fill the space between the mizzen, the mainm'st and the forem'st.

For years it was the practice among squares'l heroes to brag about the size of the vessels in which they had served. The classic response to the question: "How tall was the last ship you sailed in?" is: "I don't rightly remember just how tall, but she carried five sails above the royals."

Many of the old square-riggers carried skys'ls, which are the sails next above the royals, and I have heard of such a high falutin' thing as a "moonraker," but I doubt if these lofty handkerchiefs were of much real value, since the higher up you get, the smaller the sail has to be. The weight has to diminish proportionate to the height attained. Otherwise, you get topheavy.

The *Eagle* was not fitted with studdingsails, which are only of historical interest. A studdingsail (pronounced "stunts'l") is an additional sail on a yard set by means of a boom temporarily attached to the yard and extending outward, which provides additional sail area.

The *Eagle* does not sport skys'ls, but can still be considered rather tall. The first time I saw my men work on the royal yard, I felt like a man in the street watching window washers, wearing no safety belts, at work on the fourteenth floor. Actually, this is not a fair comparison because the

138

man on the yard has a lot of things to hold on to. He works bellied over the yard with his feet securely planted on the foot ropes. With the sails furled aloft and the yards lowered to the point where they are supported by the triangle of the topping lifts, the men looked like flies on a coat hanger when viewed from down below.

Under the routine we adopted in the beginning of the trip, our mornings started with the piling on of sail. As soon as it was good daylight, during the four to eight watch, the call would ring out:

"All hands to sail stations!"

After noses were counted as an added check against the possibility that someone may have left us during the night, the to'gallant and royal sail hands would lay aloft and loose their respective sails. The remainder of the crew would see to the jibs, stays'ls and mizzens'ls. By breakfast time, weather permitting, all sails would be set and drawing nicely, and the ship's cleaning routine could get started after chow.

The business of setting a sail comes in two phases. First, the men go aloft and cast off the gaskets, which are lashings at intervals along the yards and which fasten the folded sail in furled position. After they have shoved the bundle of sail off the top of the yard, they retreat to the safety of the deck below. It is then that the hauling begins, and lines controlling the tacks, sheets and halyards are hauled away and the sail is drawn into its working position.

The yard is set at the proper angle to the mast by means of the braces, the hauling part of which is manila line which passes through fairleads; thence along the decks. On a mechanized vessel much of this hauling is done by winches, but not on our ship. Providing the wind is steady and all the heaving and hauling is finished, the lines are coiled ready for running, but only after the hauling parts have been securely double looped around belaying pins.

139

With the sails set and drawing, the OD keeps an eye cocked aloft, watching particularly the weather half of the royal for the beginning of a slight quivering. A shaking action will indicate that he is as close to the wind as he can get.

The working day can now begin. The decks get scrubbed and the general housekeeping routine is followed until it is necessary to tack, take off sail, or get involved in some other maneuver connected with the following of our course.

In spite of my trepidation, the Bay of Biscay turned out to be tranquil. None of the fabled Biscay weather was in evidence in our radio weather reports. The main trouble was light airs. Every day we were getting further offshore and less likely to be embayed.

We passed occasional fishermen, French or Spanish. They invariably changed course and hauled over in our direction to have a better look. One night a big passenger ship, lit up like a Christmas tree, came steaming by, heading in the general direction of Gibraltar. It was a bright, clear night, and we had half a moon. I could tell by the ship's maneuvering that the captain got us between him and the moon so the passengers could have a good look at our silhouette. Only the lower courses and tops'ls were set. I was sorry we didn't have everything on so we could give them a real show.

At that moment I remembered passing a square-rigger under full sail in the moonlight, just off Havana entrance in 1925. I was on a destroyer and the romance of the moment was hard to capture with blowers running, turbines humming and the always lively motion of the tin cans. Still, it was an instant of beauty I never forgot. Now I had my chance to pass this experience on to someone else.

After the passenger vessel, we saw no more ships. We were leaving the beaten paths.

On the sixth day our calculations told us that we would
140

arrive off Funchal after dark on the seventh. Making our first landfall at night was no cause for alarm, since the approach to Funchal harbor is uncomplicated and relatively safe. There is a small inner harbor, but we would be required to remain anchored outside, since we had no cargo handling to do and no passenger traffic.

The main island of Madeira rises steeply out of the ocean and has very deep water close inshore. Funchal is on the lee side of the island, sheltered from the prevailing winds, thus offering quiet water for the anchorage. As we made our landfall, Madeira was silhouetted against the setting sun, at the close of a bright, clear, sub-tropical day. We approached downwind, and for the first time since our departure, carried full sail in the darkness. We would reach sheltered water behind the island before anchoring at Funchal. This would give the crew an opportunity to prove their skill at manning sail stations in the dark.

When the command was given: "Lay aloft, lay out and furl!" I paced the quarterdeck nervously, dreading the first cry of distress from aloft which would announce the slipping of a foot from a footrope or the losing of a hand hold. As the minutes dragged by, I could hardly resist the temptation to grab a flashlight and check on the progress of the work aloft. Common sense told me that this was an idiotic impulse, that the rays of light would blind someone and justify at least a round of swearing.

After what seemed to me to be sufficient time for the job to be done, I peeped at the illuminated dial of my wristwatch. They had been at the job only ten minutes! Remembering that the best time I had ever witnessed in a furling job was nineteen minutes (this had been on the *Danmark* with a fairly well trained crew in broad daylight in a snug harbor), I suppressed my anxiety and decided to use patience and have a little faith in the boys on the footropes.

It was a long hour but my faith was justified. The furling was buttoned up in a professional manner. Our drills were paying off. I told the Exec to head for the anchorage, and had the lookouts keep a sharp eye for a pilot boat. We started the diesel and headed in.

Funchal clings to the steep mountainside. The city almost stands on edge, presenting to the traveler a spectacular view from seaward. Tonight there was a religious festival going on in the upper part of town. Halfway up the mountainside a white church stood illuminated by floodlights. From the grounds nearby a fireworks display was in progress. The sound of the rockets and starshells floated across the glassy smooth water, their faint swishes and poppings barely audible. The countless twinkling lights of the town were reflected in the water, the double images deceiving the eye and making the judgment of distance uncertain.

This illusion of nearness is a trial to a navigator, since he gets the impression that the land silhouette stands twice as tall as it is. The inverted image of the land in the harbor brings the imaginary shoreline down to the ship's bow, and occasionally causes a nervous full speed astern bell.

The timely arrival of the pilot boat partially dispelled the dreamlike quality of the scene. Double checking our cross bearings revealed that we were still quite far offshore and must continue on into this three-dimensional wonderland of lights and velvety darkness. Toward midnight we dropped anchor at the spot pointed out by the pilot. Although we seemed to be alarmingly close to the beach, the depth was reassuring—fourteen fathoms. A check of my navigator's work on the chart showed that there was plenty of distance between us and the beach.

Knowing that a big day was in store, we turned in and, with the exception of the night watch, fell into the dreamless sleep which follows long hours of hard work.

Chapter X

In the early morning light the city of Funchal lay sleeping on the side of the mountain. The streets were deserted. Through binoculars, it appeared that even the cats and dogs were late sleepers. The pastel colors so frequently seen in sub-tropical ports were in evidence in the buildings, with their tiled roofs, ranged tier upon tier, up the steep slopes. The water retained its mirror-like quality. Looking down through the clean blues and greens, one could follow the anchor chain almost to the bottom. To seaward, an occasional great fish could be seen breaking the surface.

The harbor was almost empty of ships. Madeira had slept peacefully through the war. Across the landscape were scattered numerous resort hotels. Through the glasses we could see that many of them had boarded windows. Here and there were brilliant flashes of color where flame vine and bougainvillaea accented the fresh greenness of the lush vegetation.

On board there was a bustle of excited activity in preparation for our first contact with the Portuguese ashore. In the excitement of anticipating my official calls, I could only pick at my breakfast, thus incurring clucking disapproval from Heinz.

The crew was limited to "spy glass liberty" until after the exchange of calls between me and the local authorities. I now faced a command function totally alien to my experience.

In the leisurely years before World War II promotion was slow. Although I had fifteen years' commissioned service at the outbreak of the war I was still a junior officer. At

143

the time of Pearl Harbor, with the rank of lieutenant, I had only recently assumed my first command, and had never steamed into a foreign port in which the responsibility of representing my country rested on my shoulders. As junior officers, my shipmates and I had often watched the Captain go chugging off toward a foreign landing on the mysterious mission of paying formal calls. Somehow, the seniors never got around to telling the juniors what one did on these calls and what one said. We watched the dignitaries returning the calls, and aside from the flourish of ceremonies at the gangway, none of us knew what went on when the skipper and his visitors withdrew to the inner sanctum of the cabin. We only knew how to hustle sideboys into place and step discreetly to one side while the captain stood facing the gangway to receive the visitors.

This stop in Madeira was a new phase in the initiation of a green skipper. The urgency of the war years had set aside the formalities of peace time. I was about to re-establish one of our older service customs, and with no one to guide me.

Normally, colors would have been made at eight, but being a newly arrived foreign vessel, our national ensign was displayed at the gaff from the beginning of daylight. A few days before our arrival, we found that there was no Portuguese flag on board, and no one could recall the design. Fanning through the books in the navigator's library, we located a color plate. With the aid of the quartermaster, the German tailor had whipped up a reasonable facsimile, which now hung limply at our main truck in the morning calm. At 148 feet above the waterline, it would take a sharp eye to detect any inaccuracy in the finished product.

With the pre-breakfast routine finished, the decks scrubbed, the paint work wiped down and the brass beginning to gleam in the early morning sunlight, the deck force industriously prepared for that critical first day under the

144

A painted ship on a painted ocean.

Funchal Harbor. The smooth, tight furl makes the yards appear almost bare.

appraising eyes of the dignitaries who would visit the ship. I paced nervously across the quarterdeck awaiting the "Boarding Call," my new half-Wellington boots, acquired in Falmouth, announcing to one and all that I was dressed in my Sunday best. The hard heels clacking on the teak decks made me feel self-conscious.

Shortly after eight a messenger brought word that a boat flying a Portuguese flag was headed out from the city landing. Binoculars examined the boat anxiously as we tried to determine what manner of official was making this momentous first visit. Ranking as a visiting man-o-war, the *Eagle* should normally receive a junior naval officer, according to nautical protocol. He would come on board, pay the respects from the authorities on shore, and discreetly determine the rank of the senior man, thereby enabling his seniors to be prepared to render appropriate honors.

A dapper young Portuguese lieutenant arrived and gathered the necessary information. We, in turn, learned from him the names and ranks of the senior officials ashore. After waiting until his boat arrived at the quay, my gig was called to the gangway and I set out for the beach. All hands must remain on board until the exchanging of calls was completed.

My first visit was to the American consul. This was necessary in order to be properly briefed on the calls which were to follow. The consul was cordial, and seemed pleased to have this break in his routine. As we discussed the ship and the impending calls over coffee, he told me that our arrival was a complete surprise, since he had had no word from the State Department of our visit. This was annoying. Our application for permission to make the various ports of call had been made well in advance.

My next question was: "Should we forthwith get up anchor and leave since we were there without permission?" This would have been an awkward thing to do because we needed the topping off of our water and fuel tanks, and an additional supply of food for the three thousand mile haul to Bermuda which was to follow, to say nothing of the sharp disappointment which would be felt by all hands should we be chased out to sea. He laughingly reassured me on this score, and said that permission to call at Funchal would undoubtedly come through in a routine fashion, perhaps weeks after our departure. Madeira had been by-passed for so long during the recent war years that he was accustomed to such delays. Mail delivery, as transmitted from the outside world to Funchal was, at best, a leisurely process. There could be no airmail because there was no airport on any of the islands and the airlines were now flying land planes. In a normal routine, mail from the United States went first to Portugal and then back to Madeira.

We passed on to the next, and to me, very important part of our conversation. On whom should I call, and what special advice could he offer?

It was well that I asked because calling on the Governor General involved a tricky procedure. I was to call, in order, on the Governor General at his palace, then upon the senior army officer present, and finally on the senior naval officer, whose young aide had made the boarding call that morning. The visits to the military were routine and uncomplicated, but not so the Governor General.

It was fortunate for me that the government offices where I was to make the calls were close together and near the consulate, because I had no escudos with which to pay a taxi, and had been told by the consul that there was no way to change money, officially.

The Governor's palace was a buff-colored stucco building, dignified by iron grillwork on either side of a porte cochere entrance, obviously designed to receive visitors from vehicles only. There was no foot path. I put up a

147

brave front as I clomped up the driveway in my hard heels, but inwardly I suffered from stage fright.

The fanfare of my reception at the gate and the courteous, bowing directions extended by the receptionist at the door of the palace, told me that I was expected. My boot heels on the flagstones sent the word ahead. The Governor General's suite lay at the end of a long black and white marble flagstone hallway. The Governor's secretary greeted me at the entrance to the suite with suave polished courtesy. His English was devoid of accent. I was promptly ushered into the Governor General's presence, where I carried out the first phase of my briefing—a formal bow, in which I instinctively clicked my heels. This was an unaccustomed thing for me to do. I felt a little foolish.

The Governor General, a slight, elegant figure in his middle thirties, was a man of considerable charm. His informality quickly put me at ease. As we were seated, I gazed admiringly around the suite while he was ordering wine. There were ancient relics of old Portugal on display. Thick Oriental rugs covered the parquet floor. The atmosphere, warmed by a truly magnificent wine, was conducive to enjoyment of what might have been a stiff formality.

When I complimented him on the wine he was pleased. It was from his private cellar and was of the best obtainable. He pressed a second glass upon me. I need not have wondered at the mystery of a formal call. It was a simple piece of common sense—a friendly visit framed in a formal procedure. The visit threatened to go beyond its allotted twenty minutes. I was beginning to wonder how to manage a graceful exit when, as if by some psychic exchange of signals, the conversation reached the pause I had been awaiting. With this, I arose, expressed my pleasure at being so received, and carried out phase two.

After a warm handshake, I paused at the door and bowed

148

for the second time. Starting down the long, long corridor, I could feel the Governor's eyes boring into my back. I knew he would be there with his secretary watching my exit, because this was the way the consul had said it would be. The hall seemed endless, as I marched and marched and marched. At last I stopped, wheeled around, and there, sure enough, they stood awaiting my third bow. Even at this distance I could make out their smiles of approval. I had passed the test. With knees slightly atremble, I rounded the corner, and heaved a sigh of relief, proceeding directly to the senior army officer's office in the same building.

Here also the visit was pleasant, but our conversation was conducted through an interpreter, since the Colonel spoke no English. Once again I was offered excellent wine. In the course of the conversation I foolishly mentioned that I had studied four years of Spanish while in school. The Colonel beamed, and came at me with a flood of Spanish. Blushing with embarrassment, I retreated, mumbling something to the effect of "muchos años pasado," and "perdido," which, I hoped was saying that I had forgotten most of my Spanish.

My next host, a Navy Captain, did speak English, and expressed great interest in the *Eagle*. He had admired the ship from the beach and could hardly wait to get on board and examine her more closely. Over another glass of wine, I launched into my favorite subject, and shut off the conversation reluctantly, with what I hoped was becoming modesty, somewhere near the twenty-minute mark.

Three official calls in one day was about my limit in this hospitable country. Returning to the waterfront, I was glad I was going downhill, and walked with elaborate care for fear of slipping on the polished cobblestones. The hot mid-morning sun bore down. The humidity had increased; the blue woolen uniform felt like an overcoat.

Island hospitality, plus failure to eat breakfast, had a

149

cumulative effect. Nearing the *Eagle* in the gig, I was overcome with a sentimental admiration. Her white sides mirrored the lapping waves, stirred up by the numerous bumboats gathered around. Aloft every yard was square, a point of pride among sailormen when in port. There was no vestige of a wrinkle from the furling job of the night before. We circled the ship while I checked rigging. The job had been well done. The yards were parallel to the horizon at exact right angles to the keel. Braces and sheets were taut.

The afternoon was spent receiving return calls from the four officials visited during the morning. They arranged to arrive in succession, in descending order of rank. No sooner did one official party steam away from the side than another would be sighted in the distance. Because regulations prohibited anything alcoholic, coffee was served. Since Heinz had administered coffee as a restorative after the rigors of the morning, sharing it with each guest in turn became burdensome before the afternoon was over. I was so loaded with caffein I did not expect to sleep for a week.

When the calls were over, the ship's officers went ashore at the Consul's invitation. From his office we strolled to his home, getting our first close look at Funchal. The Consul exchanged greetings with everyone we met. The atmosphere was friendly, and the pace of life leisurely.

The Consul lived a short distance from the consulate office in a comfortable wooden house. He served us cocktails in the garden, where we had an opportunity to look at his flowers. His garden was his hobby. Rows of bearing banana trees served as a backdrop to the flowers, which ranged from exotic bird-of-paradise and orchid, to everyday pink gladiola.

Doc took a sip of his drink, gazed at the beauty around him, and remarked:

"Gosh, this is a regular Garden of Eden!"

The Consul agreed.

150

"Yes, it *is* the Garden of Eden." Pointing at the mountain, he went on:

"You can move from down here in this tropical splendor right up that slope on any day in the year and select the temperature you want. The pass at the top is over six thousand feet above sea level. You see these flowers? It takes no great effort to raise them. They seem to want to grow. We have a colony of ex-patriates—some British, some American, all delightful, well-mannered people. Any time I want a bridge game, bridge is welcome. The food is good here. We have the best of meats, seafoods and wines. There is never any winter, and no summer. The northeast trade winds see to that. I can't see anything wrong with the place at all. I've had nine years of perfection—and I'm sick of it!"

On the first day bumboats surrounded the ship. The second day they were even more numerous. The war had been hard on bumboatmen and they were eager for business. For that part of the crew who must remain on board and stand watches, the bumboatmen provide a real service. They bring a multitude of products of the land and sell for the best price they can command. They seem to abound primarily in tropical harbors.

Watching their efforts to get attention to their wares, I was reminded of the hawking of Cuban bumboatmen, who always carried a bottle of rum concealed in their innocent appearing baskets, and would take a chance on a quick transaction through an open airport. The Madeira bumboatmen offered a wide variety of things, including poor examples of the famous Madeira linens, fruit, vegetables, canary birds, assorted junk, and wine in bottles, jugs, kegs, or any container that would hold a stopper.

On the second morning there were so many of them that the competition threatened to kill off profits. To keep illicit cargo from coming on board, fire hoses were led out forward and aft, and streams of water played along the ship's sides.

This is a standard defense against the bumboatman after a fast buck. Bowing to the inevitable, the boatmen sent a small delegation on board armed with credentials in the form of noncommittal testimonials, purportedly written by officers of ships which had previously visited the harbor. It was agreed that a selected few, nominated by the whole group, would be allowed to come on board and lay out their goods on a cleared area of the quarterdeck under the watchful eyes of the officer of the deck and the quartermaster. This arrangement seemed to please all concerned, and peace of a confused sort reigned.

The Governor General had invited the ship's officers to a picnic. Those who could be spared from the day's routine went ashore. We were met at the palace entrance by the Governor and his staff. The first view of an impressive motorcade drawn up in front made it clear that this "picnic" was going to be quite a party. We piled into the cars, the Chief of Police of the island and some of his lieutenants in the leading car, the Governor General, a visiting British naval officer and I in the second car. The rest of the guests distributed themselves in the remainder of the caravan.

With the uproar of continually tooting horns, we set off at a frighteningly fast clip in the general direction of the mountains back of the city. We went roaring up a steep grade and skidded around a hairpin turn, the tires squealing in protest. With a clash of shifting gears, this process was repeated. Up, and up. We gained altitude fast. I looked toward the harbor. Far below was a toy ship—my *Eagle*.

Down in town it had been a bright, hot day. As we climbed it got cool, then cold, and near the top teeth were chattering with the chill. A light cover of clouds hung over the mountain pass, mercifully obscuring the awesome view. I sighed with relief as we began a gentle descent along a road of wide sweeping turns, much more to my liking. When we burst into sunlight, we were in another world.

Before us was the blue Atlantic, pinpointed in the morning sunlight by sparkling whitecaps. Below lay the mosaic pattern of Portuguese farmlands. Although the hills were precipitous, they were covered with producing crops. There were vineyards and potato fields, and other crops which were unidentifiable in the distance. The contour terraces, wandering snakelike along the mountainside, rose, tier upon tier, like giant green sea waves frozen into immobility.

The Governor remarked that from here one could count the cows. I looked all about me and could see no cows. Choosing a farm at random, he pointed out a tiny gray stone house with a gabled roof, and said that each such house contained a cow. As we passed nearby I could see that the house was hardly larger than one animal. He explained that this is a form of tenderizing the beef. The cow, or steer, is imprisoned and hand fed, the lack of exercise producing beef of the desired quality.

Our trip had taken us directly across the island from south to north. As we coasted down to sea level, we slanted eastward, where the road followed the shoreline. The rugged terrain gave way to gently rolling hills.

Near the eastern tip of the island we arrived at the scene of the picnic. We entered the grounds through a rustic arch overgrown with rambler roses. The driveway wound through well-tended grounds. We dismounted near a lodge and started a stroll through the gardens. We were served cocktails on the lawn, surrounded with tropical flowers.

After cocktails, we trooped into the main building, where we were shown into a large banquet hall. In front of each guest stood a tiny flag of his nationality. The meal followed formal lines. The first course consisted of an enormous poached fish of a species unknown to me. It had the general appearance of a large-mouth bass, but must have weighed as much as twenty pounds. When the meat course came on I saw the results of the stone house tenderizing. It was

153

delicate in texture, but somewhat softer than our American beef. My filet mignon was big enough for two people. The rest of the meal fades from memory in a gentle haze of gastronomic appreciation.

My well-fed complacency was interrupted by the unsettling news that a toast and a speech were expected of each guest. The Governor General set the pace by toasting the President of the United States and the King of England. A moment of panic came with the thought that I didn't know who ruled Portugal. The panic was relieved when the Consul arose, and as the senior U.S. representative, gave the required toast. My speech consisted of my best assortment of platitudes.

Back to the ship just in time to prepare for a small dinner party which had been planned for the Governor General, the American Consul and some of his friends. The Governor General had earlier said that he would not be able to make it due to a previous commitment, but along with his regrets he sent a bottle of his choicest Madeira wine. The wine was classified as a piece of official business, and the regulations were satisfied by having it locked up.

When the guests left, I took a few turns around the quarterdeck, reflecting on the events of the day. Gradually I became aware of the night. Strains of music floated across the moonlit harbor. At a seaside cafe near the city wharf the islanders were gathered for an after-dinner brandy. I could make out the colorful umbrellas, each marking a table where families sat together in quiet conversation, illuminated from behind by the lights of the city. A silvery path of moonlight led from ship to shore. Here and there pleasure boats drifted through the brightness and were sharply silhouetted for a moment.

My thoughts began to stray to the business of tomorrow when we would be preparing for sea.

154

Chapter XI

In Germany and England supplies and fuel could be obtained by signing a receipt in the name of the United States Navy. In Madeira we were on our own. Von had lined up sources of water and food, but it was my problem to find a way to pay for them.

I went into a huddle with the Consul. He came up with the suggestion that I obtain bills in triplicate from all the suppliers and sign voucher forms against the indebtedness. Armed with this commitment, he would persuade the merchants to deliver the necessary stores, and would send the vouchers into Washington through State Department channels, where they would eventually be presented to my Headquarters for settlement. Hoping there was nothing fatally illegal in this procedure, I meekly signed everything that was laid before me, and the loading proceeded.

The topping off of tanks and fattening of our food supply was necessary in face of the route chosen. The next leg of the trip was to be a three thousand mile arc to Bermuda, following fair breeze and current.

At dawn the signal to weigh anchor was given, and the high-spirited boys at the capstan bars started their merry whirl 'round and 'round the anchor windlass. All the way aft could be heard the thump, thump, thumping of their feet against the cleats. The merry-go-round performance on the fo'castle went on and on. I waited impatiently for the "short stay" signal. (The anchor is at "short stay" when all the chain is in except a little more than the depth of the water. Any further heaving will break the anchor from its holding on the bottom.) We had about fifty

155

fathoms of chain out in fourteen fathoms of water. Surely we must have heaved in at least forty fathoms of chain by now! The anchor gang began to lose its enthusiasm, and the cadence of their tramping slowed noticeably. The Exec called forward and asked how much chain remained outside the hawse pipes. The answer came back:

"Thirty fathoms!"

Only twenty fathoms, and the boys were beginning to puff and sweat! More men were sent to the fo'castle to relieve the tiring laborers. I went forward to have a look as the new gang took over and speeded up the progress of the windlass.

I was familiar with the workings of the hand powered machine but had not realized what an extremely high gear ratio was necessary to get our more than three thousand pounds of anchor in by muscles alone. While the gang was puffing 'round and 'round at a mighty clip, the anchor chain was creeping in at a snail's pace. This departure was going to be anything but a snappy affair.

While the drudgery was going on Ka-Leut sidled up with a suggestion:

"Cap-tain, in this very hard work we haf music sometimes and the men do not get so tired. Maybe one man sits on the windlass and plays the concertina. Then the men sing while they work and forget about being tired."

"Ka-Leut, I wish we had time for that. I think music would help, but my men are not accustomed to working that way."

I had no intention of teaching sea chanties to the crew at this stage in the game.

At the end of two gruelling hours, when the anchor was finally catted and secured on the billboard, the crew flopped on deck and panted for breath. There would be no manning of sail stations. There was no breeze, for which they were grateful. In the wind shadow of the island we

156

were totally becalmed. It would have been nice to put on a display for our new friends ashore, but we were forced to putt-putt ignominiously into the distance under bare poles.

A full half day went by while we were steaming out from under the six thousand foot windbreaker that is Madeira. It was late afternoon before we were able to gather enough of the trade winds to justify making sail. As the *Eagle* chugged along, the mountains grew fainter in outline while still above the horizon. They changed from deep green gently through the spectrum, to hazy blue, and melted into the nothingness of the pale sky beyond.

Since the rigging had received a sufficient shakedown on the passage to Madeira, we could now put on and take off sail without fear of embarrassment. The crew had graduated from sailing kindergarten the night we arrived at Funchal. With complete confidence in the trade wind and the season, I decided that there would be no more timid shortening of sail at night unless conditions changed, and so specified in the night order book. This carrying of full sail around the clock extended my night owl tendency.

The next morning Doc came out on deck, blinked at the bright sky, stared briefly and disinterestedly at the dancing whitecaps on the gulf stream blue of the water, collapsed into a deck chair and held his head in his hands. It occurred to me that I had not seen Doc since the day we arrived in Madeira.

"What on earth's wrong, Doc? And, incidentally, where have you been for the past three days?"

"Oh, I've just been playing the fool. I took a room at the hotel up on the cliff and tried to buy the island out while we were there. I found a place that would cash my checks and just about cleaned out my account at home. I'm going to have some tall explaining to do when I see my wife."

"You've got plenty of company, Doc. Probably every

American on board did the same thing. The only thing that kept me from joining the shopping mob was press of official business. Even so, I bought a bunch of junk that my wife will probably dispose of as soon as she can gracefully do so. I even bought some of the junk brought out by the bumboatmen."

Doc's depression continued until the second day, when another man developed a toothache. This raised his morale and brought the sparkle back to his eye.

By noon of the second day the breeze approached the ideal—just strong enough for a lively eight knots tacking diagonally downwind (This maneuver is actually "wearing," first to starboard and then to port, just enough to keep all sails filled and drawing nicely), but not strong enough to build a sea of any size.

The trade wind sky is a greenish blue, relieved from monotony by lamb's wool puffs of cloud. Along the ocean's ruffled highway marched legions of young whitecaps in orderly rows. Our tall ship swept along in silence, like a queen in full regalia, moving among her bowing subjects to the coronation ceremony.

The pilot charts show that this area of ocean is almost never crossed by steamship lanes. Fortunately for us, these charts still carry sailing ship routes, although this information is practically archaic. As day followed mint-bright day freshly coined from the good weather locker, we saw no other ships. Not a solitary vessel was sighted from Madeira to Bermuda.

The day after leaving Madeira our galley served up fish which had been purchased locally. My cabin guests and I had never tasted anything quite so good, and sent Heinz back to the galley to get seconds. That afternoon I remarked to Von that it was the best fish I had ever eaten, and I was hoping that he had laid in a good supply.

He grinned.

158

"Cap'n, you aren't the only one who liked that fish. The crew went plumb wild. I thought I had laid in a supply for at least three feedings, but it was a bum guess. You know, sailors usually go easy on fish, and if they gripe at all on a ship, it will be on a Friday—but not this bunch of pelicans. They got next to the cooks and those soft-hearted clucks cooked up every last bit of it. It's all gone."

"What kind of fish was it, Von?"

"Darned if I know, Cap'n. I never saw anything like it before. It was a long, slender fish almost like an eel and I didn't much like the looks of it, but took the dealer's word that it was the best fish in Madeira, and it sure was."

The whole trip seemed to be involved in the discovery of new kinds of fish. On my side trip to Copenhagen I had been served a variety of pink spotted flounder, or sole, in the famous D'Angleterre Hotel. It had been of such delicate texture that it almost had to be eaten with a spoon. At the time I had pronounced it fit for the gods. Then again, I was reminded of the time when Ka-Leut's fishermen friends had brought a marvelous catch in from the North Sea. This was equally good, but the fish was a total stranger to me. The next step was the enormous specimen on the table at the picnic in Madeira.

This fish parade was truly exceptional, or my taste had changed since, in true sailor fashion, I had never been fond of fish. I harked back to the time when I first began to view seafood with a jaundiced eye. During the ice patrol season of 1925-26 my cutter had often spoken French fishermen on the Grand Banks of Newfoundland. Each time we would offer to take their mail into Halifax, where it would be sent back to the Gascony Coast from which they operated, their gratitude for this small act was expressed in the form of whole boatloads of fish, usually cod. An economy-minded commissary officer brought forth a flood of griping by feeding us the stuff day after day until we showed signs of incipient revolt.

With each day becoming successively better weatherwise than the one before, and our being spared the necessity of working the ship by beating to windward, we devoted our attention to getting all shined up for an eventual triumphant arrival at home. During the war all brass and bright work had been painted over and our overhaul had not permitted the luxury of uncovering the bright work. Now we made a game of discovering brass and shining it, and of laying bare velvety brown areas of teak and applying the satiny finish this handsome wood deserves.

By scratching painted surfaces with the tip of a knife blade, our prospecting was rewarded with rich strikes. The pelorus stands on the port and starboard quarterdeck railings turned out to be solid brass. So did the ventilator tops. Brass trimmings were found all about the quarterdeck. For once, I saw sailors shining brass and looking as though they liked it. Each day we became shinier and smarter in appearance. Even the old sails seemed to take on new life with the bleaching effect of the strong tropical sun.

The only jarring note was a young epidemic of sunburn among the inexperienced who were in too much of a hurry to acquire the bronzed look of the real sailorman. Knowing my weakness—a tendency to burn easily—I took a gingerly approach and increased my exposure to the sun in daily increments of five minutes. At the end of a week all hands could safely wear the uniform of the day—sneakers, swim trunks and a hat.

This was about the most unmilitary man-o-war that ever floated. The only drills held were the ones necessary for the protection of the ship and crew on the passage. Fire, collision, abandon ship and man overboard drills are ordinary precautions which must not be neglected on any ship.

160

All other effort was directed toward obtaining smartness and the proper operation of the running rigging.

Our watch, quarter and station bill was like no other I had ever seen. The bill usually takes the form of a large white poster mounted under glass at some convenient spot easily accessible to the crew. Across the top are listed the various types of drills, such as fire, collision, man overboard, etc. Down the left hand side appear a series of numbers and the names of the crew. If a new man desires to find out what his duties are at, for example, fire drill, he goes to the station bill, finds his name and runs across the ruled column until he comes to the section headed "Fire Drill." There he will find his duties spelled out. If he is one of a group of seamen, all of whom are assigned to a similar task, such as the manning of fire hose No. 1, he will find this designation under the first seaman listed, and those underneath indicated by ditto marks.

Our station bill had to take into account the extraordinary nature of the ship and include such details as the sail stations to be manned at emergency drills. In the preparation of our station bill I noticed the executive officer using the letters "D O" instead of "DITTO." I told him to erase it and spell out the word "ditto," because I did not want a repetition of a scene I had witnessed many years ago.

When I was a rosy-cheeked beginner in the fo'castle I had pored over the ship's bill, memorizing my own duties fairly well, but I had a shipmate, a wardroom mess attendant from the deep South, who did not fully understand everything he saw. The first time we held an emergency fire drill he was observed by his division officer wandering aimlessly about the deck.

"What are your duties at fire drill, lad?"

"Ah do-no, suh."

"Have you looked at the watch, quarter and station bill?"

161

"Yas, suh."

"And you still don't know?"

"Naw, suh."

"Well, go look now and report back to me."

After a wait of fully fifteen minutes, the victim shuffled up to his inquisitor and hung his head in silence.

"Well, what did it say?"

"Hit say 'do', but hit don't say *what* to do."

As we settled comfortably into our suntan, the days took on a repetitious sameness of serenity and well ordered work. Had it not been for the little variations of human nature, dullness might have set in. Long days at sea have a way of exaggerating the personal peculiarities of shipmates. The isolation of shipboard life magnifies the importance of small things which might go unnoticed ashore.

We had taken on a supply of deck chairs before starting the trip, and had them distributed around in various parts of the vessel where they would not get in the way of ship's work. Anyone not on watch or on the duty section for deck work was free to do as he chose in the way of recreation. On the welldeck around the forem'st and mainm'st someone was always frolicking about with one of the puppies. The puppies were flourishing, but the canary birds the crew had bought in Madeira turned out to be a short term purchase. At the halfway point they had all passed away. They had been a splendid collection of mutes; not one let out a peep the entire time he (or she) was on board.

My private reservation was a corner of the quarterdeck alongside the radio shack, where my personal deck chair was set up. The chair was plainly marked. I kept irregular hours, but occasionally showed up at my playground for a sunbath. All hands respected the holy ground, except the irrepressible chief engineer. My irritation at seeing him perched in my chair was unreasoning. I could not imagine myself getting burned up over such a small

162

thing. There was plenty of room and chairs for everyone. I could feel my irritation mounting and wondered that it did not show in my face, but he invariably greeted me with an affectionate smile, all wide-eyed innocence. It was such a petty affair I was ashamed to give him a growl; at the same time, I devoutly wished he would get some sense through that thick head of his and recognize the "Captain's prerogatives."

Some days after he had started monopolizing my spot, he hopped to attention when I appeared and apologized for taking the Captain's chair. I felt ridiculous because the silly thing had taken on such importance. Perhaps one of the other officers had sensed my feelings and had quietly shown him the light. For the rest of the trip no one trespassed.

The chief engineer also had his odd quirk. His purchases in Funchal, in addition to the inevitable canary birds, consisted largely of living plants of every description. In spite of our warnings that the Department of Agriculture would not permit growing plants to land in the United States, he had kept on buying until his room looked like a greenhouse. There were flower pots, window boxes and an assortment of containers sitting in baskets, buckets, even the lavatory washbowl. He seemed to have a childlike faith in the possibility that the laws governing the import of foreign vegetation might be repealed by the time we got home.

He was approaching retirement. Since most seagoing men seem to have a longing for farm life to the point of downright nearsightedness considering the drudgery involved in such a life, this collecting of greenery must have been dictated by his sub-conscious wishes. All of his off-duty time, except that spent in sun bathing, was devoted to his precious plants. I didn't see a blossom among the whole tangled mass when I peeped in to have a look at his conservatory. I was to later witness a burial at sea at the hands of the officials at the quarantine anchorage in the States, while the chief watched the ruthless slaughter in almost tearful sorrow.

As his hobby, Doc took up the study of celestial navigation, while he mentally wielded a scalpel in preparation for a dramatic piece of impromptu surgery.

Some of the crew worked systematically through the collection of reading matter which had been thoughtfully put on board by the Red Cross just before we sailed. A few poor souls shifted their brains into neutral, and for hours on end, sat gazing into space with a vacant stare.

The Germans kept pretty much to themselves when off duty, but they seemed to be having a high old time. Sounds of singing poured forth through the ventilators from their quarters below. Their withdrawal had no resemblance to clannishness or coolness toward the Americans. Throughout the watches I could see signs of budding friendships between the two nationalities, but the language barrier imposes restraint in human relationships, even in the presence of mutual trust and friendship.

I could feel this slight restraint in my relations with Ka-Leut, in spite of the fact that by now his English had become near perfect. I believe the barrier finally disappears when one national can think in the other's language and the other can, in turn, do so in the language he has acquired.

Our food supply was adequate, our water fresh and sweet. We were having none of the privations so common in tales told of old square-riggers. With a fair breeze twenty-four hours a day and no prospect of change, the business of sailing was pure pleasure without the accentuating influence of intermittent hardship. There was no breaking out of the watch below for reefing or furling, no wild activity of howling storm. The only scrambling aloft was for the exercise and drill value.

As we sat sunning ourselves, lightly clad, sprawled in

164

deck chairs and enjoying the motion of the ship, all seemed right with the world. We wore out the expression—"Some people pay big money to do this."

A stop in the Canary Islands as originally planned, would not have caused much delay because we came within easy striking distance before we turned westward. In our lazy discussions while basking in the sun, we agreed that Columbus was shot with luck. Once into the northeast trades at about latitude 23-30 north, just hold the prevailing breeze and you can't help discovering America.

In the vicinity of the Canary Islands the trade winds curve to the westward and follow the equator. Since we were making pretty good time—about two hundred miles a day—we decided to vary our latitude up and down a bit and find out where the best breezes were. As we slanted southward, the breeze began to slacken around latitude 22. On reversing the process, we began to lose it again in latitude 24. With this matter settled, I chose the halfway point and continued westward under ideal conditions. Our navigational sights showed that the current was helping as well as the breeze. This course was splitting the difference between the Doldrums and the Horse Latitudes, both of which are to be avoided.

The Doldrums, depending upon the season, generally lie between latitude 20 and the equator, both north and south, and because of frequent calms and capricious light airs, plagued the lives of sailormen since they first ventured fearfully away from the coasts of Europe and Africa.

The Horse Latitudes are a broad band of the same kind of weather, running generally east and west, in the vicinity of latitude 30 north and 30 south, or so the books say. The story goes that in the early days sailing ships carrying horses in their cargo would run low in water, and the combination of the blazing sun and the shortage of water would kill the horses. Some old sea stories have told of ships coming upon

165

the bloated carcasses floating on the surface, dumped over-board from another luckless vessel which had lost her sailing breeze for too many days. ENCYCLOPEDIA BRITTANICA carries a short paragraph under "Horse Latitudes" stating that this yarn is without foundation, but offers no suitable origin of its own for the colorful expression. I choose to believe the old sailors' account.

If curiosity about people and things can keep one young, Doc will never grow old. The art of navigation gained an acolyte early in the trip when he was watching the navigator take evening star sights. He pestered him until each step of the process had been explained. With the Exec's permission, he adopted one of our numerous sextants as his own for the trip, and learned how to take an altitude in a short time.

With modern navigational methods, the process of solving the astronomical triangle is relatively simple provided the student is instructed in the use of the Nautical Almanac, the tables of computation, and has a working knowledge of astronomical time as applied in navigation. By the end of a week after we left Madeira, Doc was getting solutions of a sort from his observations. At trip's end the navigator pronounced him competent to do a fairly good "day's work." I wondered what turn his restless mind would take next.

In the midst of Doc's exploration of his new hobby, there arose a situation which temporarily distracted him. A messenger brought word that Ka-Leut and the German doctor wanted to see me on an urgent matter. At about the halfway point between Madeira and Bermuda one of the American crewmen showed positive symptoms of acute appendicitis. Now I had the situation I had dreaded at the beginning of the trip! After a long discussion with the German doctor and Ka-Leut, we agreed that the doctor should watch the patient for another twenty-four hours, with special vigilance on his blood count, temperature, and the localized pain. At the time the count was rising, and ice packs had already been applied and penicillin administered.

Doc almost chortled with glee upon hearing the bad news. Here was his Big Chance. He ostentatiously took his seat on the quarterdeck and began pawing through a volume on surgery and another on anatomy.

With a silent prayer, I settled into my chair and tried to ignore his studious exploration in the field of surgery. Almost, I wished he had not been on board. It just added complications to the picture. Things would have been easier if there had been only the German surgeon to rely on, without this ambitious dilettante in my hair.

During the first few hours of our crisis, I kept Ka-Leut running back and forth to the sick bay for the latest word from his doctor, who was maintaining a constant vigil. As Ka-Leut would come up to make his report I rather pointedly walked to a spot out of earshot of our would-be surgeon.

"What is the latest blood count?"

"12,000, Cap-tain."

"What was it last time?"

"Between 11 and 12, sir."

"Still rising, eh?"

"Yes, sir. The doctor says that if the count gets to 13,000, operation will be necessary."

One thing was in our favor. We could hold a course with an absolutely dependable breeze and the ship would be steady as a rock. Our generators were working normally, and if the operation became necessary we would have plenty of light. The truth is I had made my decision, but this challenging situation was so stimulating to Doc that my main problem was going to be breaking the news to him if and when an operation was forced upon us. I was probably going to have to lock the enthusiastic cuss in his room while the German doctor performed the duty for which he had been trained.

As the blood count mounted, tension kept pace. I had trouble avoiding Doc, whose company I usually enjoyed. He made a great show of his fussing about with preparations for his big moment.

After about ten hours of our shipboard drama, Ka-Leut brought momentous news. The blood count had leveled off and held steady, and his temperature had abated. Three more hours and the count turned downward. By the following morning the boy seemed to be almost normal. In another day he was back at work. A tiny private cloud of gloom hung over the head of Doc, the frustrated surgeon.

This development was accompanied by a pleasanter one. The German boy with the incurable wound suddenly began to recover. Ka-Leut marched him up to me and happily had him show that the lesion was almost gone. This seemed fairly conclusive proof that the right food in sufficient quantity and the good sea life was what the boy had needed, and that Mother Nature unhindered was now performing the miracle which had been denied to medical science in Germany. By the time we reached New York the wound was fully healed and the boy in perfect health.

Our good sailing weather had to end sometime. The pilot charts showed that this beautiful breeze could be held all the way to St. Thomas, Virgin Islands, as had been the original plan, but by cutting the trip short, we had to leave the trade winds and head diagonally toward Bermuda. Our problem was to select a point where this could be done most economically in time. We could hold our westward course (and the breeze) until it would be necessary to make a ninety-degree course change. Or, we could start slanting northward while still some distance out, and gamble on holding a breeze of sorts all the way.

The navigator and I, having nothing better to influence

the decision, agreed that about a forty-five degree change of course would probably be as good as any other. This would put us on the hypotenuse of a right triangle. With three days' sailing estimated to get us into Hamilton harbor, the change of course was made.

Our breeze continued for a day and a half, at which time it died abruptly. We had entered the Horse Latitudes, which must be crossed at one point or another in order to get to Bermuda.

After the breeze failed we were like a "painted ship upon a painted ocean."

"Start the engine!"

The *Eagle* chugged mournfully along with everything furled in an empty ocean. Her wake followed a perspective line on the liquid mirror to the vanishing point astern. The smooth ripples of her bow wave made a perfect V, extending to either quarter beyond the range of sight. The world was standing still and wind no longer existed. Cumulus clouds hung motionless in the distance with perfect inverted images below, their expanding towers and battlements finally reaching the stratosphere, where they shaped into gigantic anvils. Somewhere below these distant displays there would be rain squalls, possibly with some wind. The air had taken on a crystal quality that made the clouds seem hundreds of miles away.

The barometer told us that we were well into the area of fairly constant high pressure near Bermuda. I was reasonably certain that for a while at least nothing but dry clear calm weather could be expected, and resigned myself to the fate of chugging into Hamilton harbor with everything furled. That is what happened. We had no more breeze and set no more sail for this leg of the trip.

Having some time to kill in order to properly arrive off St. David's Head at the entrance to the channel leading into Hamilton at dawn the next day, I decided to fool

169

around a bit. This gave us a chance to experiment and gather performance data of various kinds. Here was an opportunity to determine the size of the ship's turning circle and to measure the "advance" and "transfer."

"Advance" means the distance a ship will travel along the line of her original course after the rudder has been suddenly put full over. "Transfer" is the movement a ship will make sidewise under the same conditions until she reaches a heading ninety degrees from her original course. This is useful information when handling a ship in harbors and in maneuvering generally.

The day before making a landfall the ship began running through large patches of Sargasso weed. This area is, in fact, the edge of the Sargasso Sea. Knowing that fish are usually to be found around this yellow-brown floating vegetation, I performed an independent experiment. Having the Exec steer close to one of the large patches, I trolled a Japanese feather lure past the tip of the mass of weeds.

Bang—I had a strike!

Yelling, "Stop the engine!" I settled down to the problem of getting my prize on board. It was a 25-pound wahoo. He put up a terrific fight but luck was with me. I had not had the pleasure of catching a wahoo before. Once again on this trip I met a new fish.

Then came a dolphin, the golden-green race horse of the sea. He comes on board vividly colored, still gasping and fighting for his life-giving element, and while he lies dying, the colors die with him. It is a spectacular and tragic thing to see. After watching this, I lost my taste for fishing, and gave the order to resume course and speed.

Next day at the crack of dawn, just as the navigator (and Doc) had predicted, we made our landfall.

Chapter XII

We picked up the pilot and started in toward Hamilton harbor. The early morning light grew brighter and removed the mystery of the ghostly headlands as we weaved our way along the tortuous channel from St. David's Head. These waters are undefiled by the silt of creeks or rivers and remain startlingly transparent, except for the brief intervals following the rare visits of tropical hurricanes, when the coral dust is churned up from the bottom, giving the waters a pearly opalescence.

A first visit to Bermuda tries the nerves of a navigator. The quality of the water creates an illusion of extreme shallowness, bringing the certainty that grounding is imminent while there is still a comfortable ten fathoms under the keel. Having visited Bermuda before, I was prepared for this, and relied upon the certainties of the fixed beacons for my piloting. The presence of the pilot in no way relieved me of my responsibility as commanding officer. Nevertheless, I restrained my tendency to meddle with this expert on our inward passage.

The pilot was going to take us far down the bay to the U.S. Naval anchorage, since he believed the *Eagle* to be an American Navy ship. I set him right by pointing aloft to the Coast Guard ensign. (The law provides that the Coast Guard shall become a part of the Navy in time of war or when the President so directs. At other times it is an arm of the Treasury Department, but, paradoxically, is always one of the armed forces. After serving as part of the Navy for the duration of World War II, the Coast Guard was returned to the Treasury Department on January 1, 1946.)

I selected a desirable spot smack-dab in the middle of Hamilton harbor, just to one side of the main channel. This gave us an excellent view on all sides and, incidentally, showed us off to advantage to all eyes ashore. Shaking his head at my boldness in commandeering the choicest spot in the harbor, the pilot went ashore.

The work permitted by the long bright days of our passage was reflected in our appearance. The *Eagle* was in tiptop condition. Our decks were spotless, the varnish work fore and aft accented by gleaming brass. Stages were rigged over the sides and the crew swarmed over the railings making last minute touches to the hull between the scuppers and water-line. Here and there tiny fragments of rust, the price a ship must pay for wearing white at sea, were carefully erased and spotted with quick drying red lead. Before noon these red blemishes would be covered over and the ship's sides would be restored to snowy perfection.

I set off on my round of calls. The call on the U.S. Consul General was short and sweet. Here I learned that a call on the British Military and Naval forces would not be required because of the presence in Bermuda of the U.S. Navy. A military call from a foreign man-o-war or from a group of vessels is a one shot affair, and is performed by the senior officer of the nationality represented.

The visit to the residence of the Governor General consisted of the signing of a guest book in his outer office. I was back on board in something less than two hours. The whole day lay before the ship's company for sightseeing and shopping. I granted liberty to the crew, and set out by motor boat to call on the senior U.S. Naval officer present.

The Navy Base was far down the bay, removed from any of the colorful region so dear to the heart of the tourist. I was received by the Admiral and here "learned" that I had pulled a boner by not taking the ship to the Navy anchorage. Pleading ignorance of the local requirements,

I told the Chief-of-Staff that since I had been cleared by the State Department for entry into Hamilton harbor, in the absence of directions to the contrary, that was where we had gone. With a cordial invitation to the naval forces to visit my unusual ship, I returned to the *Eagle*.

While calling upon the Consul General, I had broached the subject of getting my German boys ashore so that they could stretch their legs. The poor devils had served faithfully over a matter of weeks without once setting foot on the beach, and they deserved some form of relaxation and change. The suggestion was turned deftly aside. The diplomats ashore envisioned all kinds of complications if my "Nazis" were to come in contact with the local people.

By this time strong friendships had grown up between us and the Germans. In the confinement of a ship at sea this was one of the two possible inevitable developments; we would either have been blessed with the harmony which now existed, or the two groups would have been at each others' throats. The Germans took the bad news without a flicker of resentment, and carried on as though nothing had happened.

My disappointment was keener because I could not make the people ashore understand that my Germans were not rabid Nazis. Every last one of them had been carefully screened by Naval Intelligence prior to our sailing. Had any evidence of taint been found in their backgrounds, they would not have been brought along. I had explained that these men were not, and had never been, prisoners. Every man was a volunteer. All I asked was permission to select an isolated piece of beach for their recreation, but the matter was evaded and left unresolved, until I realized that my efforts were fruitless.

In all fairness, I had to admit that I was literally quivering with suspicion and distrust upon arriving in Germany, and had come by my present attitude in easy stages. Nevertheless, I found it hard to keep down my anger when a brash newspaper woman drew alongside in a rowboat and questioned me about "those Nazis you've got on board."

The Coast Guard cadet practice cruise vessel was due in Bermuda the following day. This was a mixed blessing. I felt sure my Admiral would be pleased with the appearance of the *Eagle*. Was he going to also approve of the mixed crew and the lack of military spit-and-polish? With the vessel lying safely at anchor, perhaps he would not see enough action for us to worry over this point.

In port our shortage of manpower was not evident. If the ship had been fully manned with a normal complement of something over 200, all sails could be set simultaneously man-o-war fashion, which is a beautiful maneuver to watch. As matters stood, we set sails one at a time and furled in the same way. I remembered the *Danmark* in New London and how she would boom into port under full sail, round up at an anchorage, while her sails would all disappear as by magic. No doubt the *Danmark's* performance was fresh in the Admiral's memory and we would suffer by comparison.

Early next morning the cruise cutter arrived on schedule. She crossed the bay far astern of us and headed for the Navy anchorage. I lit out in pursuit in my motor boat, with the German boat's crew. This was a deliberate piece of showmanship for the benefit of the gang on the cutter.

Germany's boat's crews are impressive to the eye. Ka-Leut had brought a good team with him. Their German Navy uniforms had somehow survived and were in excellent condition. The German sailor wears a flat hat with two trailing ribbons down the back, a short, snug fitting jacket with brass buttons, oversize broad collar similar to that worn by the British, and voluminous trousers, which are much more generous in cut than the American Blue-jacket wears. As I boarded the boat and seated myself on

174

the immaculate boat cloth, which had been hand knotted by the sailmaker as a pastime on our crossing, the bow hook and the stern hook stood stiffly erect with feet wide apart, each man with his boat hook held vertically in front of his nose, with the butt resting on deck. The coxswain stood at attention in the stern sheets and manipulated the tiller with his knees.

We made a sweeping turn away from the gangway, and with cap ribbons fluttering in the breeze, headed for the flagship. This was fancy stuff. We caught up with the cruise vessel just after she had anchored. The way the cadets and crew lined her rails satisfied me that we were attracting the desired attention. This crowd had freshly put to sea. Noses were peeled and marks of new sunburn showed plainly in every face, whereas we of the *Eagle* were all the color of seasoned mahogany.

As I mounted the companion ladder I became suddenly ill at ease at the prospect of seeing my Admiral after six and a half months of absence, and the anticipation of his judgment of our prize of war.

"Come in, McGowan. Glad to see you. You look fine. Coffee?"

This was barely a question. On visits of this kind coffee appears automatically.

"How did the job go?"

"Well, sir, you know from our correspondence what a rough time we had getting the stuff we needed. My crowd did so much scrounging and crafty requisitioning that I'm afraid I am not to be trusted from now on."

"I think we had a pretty good idea of what you were up against. From my first impression across the harbor, it looks like you made out pretty well."

As I went on to tell about some of our scheming and improvising to get the ship on her way, my stage fright disappeared.

175

"How was your crossing?"

"Admiral, aside from a nasty head wind and cold dampness in the Channel, we have had a perfect trip."

Rapping lightly on the arm of a bent oak chair,

"We've had no accidents, no injuries, and while we had the breeze we made clipper ship time. I had one boy come down with a hot appendix, but he responded to treatment without operation and was back on his feet before we got in."

At this point I wondered what my answer would be if it occurred to him to ask how we managed to have a half German crew. I was spared this in his enthusiastic questions about how the *Eagle* behaved at sea under sail. Mysteriously enough, I have never had to answer that question.

Since the Admiral had shown so much interest in my ship, I returned the compliment.

"Isn't this ship brand new, Admiral? I don't remember seeing anything like this before."

His smile disappeared.

"Yes, just commissioned. Look around you. This is a so-called 'cabin.' "

Pipe lines, air ducts and electrical cables led fore and aft and athwartships overhead. The pipes bore the regulation identification colors in a modern, efficient manner, without consideration of aesthetic sensibilities. In the older ships these necessary ship's entrails would have been discreetly concealed behind the smooth surfaces of panelling. This, no doubt, was a forward step in efficiency, but to the Admiral it was an ugly mess. The last vestige of cabin elegance had been cast aside in the interest of operational integrity. The cabin was miniature and crowded.

Mentally comparing his quarters with mine, I could think of nothing to say. The pause in our talk became overlong, and I terminated the call.

Barely had I reached my cabin after returning to the

Eagle when the Admiral's boat was reported in the offing. We fell in at the gangway with the proper number of side-boys, and my excellent boatswain's mate—one of the old school who knew the technique of blowing a pipe—first piped the boat alongside and then piped our distinguished guest over the gangway. His broad grin of appreciation over the rightness of the procedure gave me a warm glow of satisfaction.

As we reached the cabin door he stopped dead. In aston-ishment he gazed slowly around the room. Feasting his eyes on the lustrous mahogany bulkhead, nodding with approval at the gentle sculptured curves where there nor-mally would have been sharp, angular corners, he sank into the depths of my favorite leather upholstered chair. I could read his thoughts. This was to be his home next summer when the cadets set out on their annual cruise.

This part of the inspection, for which I could take no credit, was a roaring success. Following up my advantage, I flung open the doors of the bedroom and dining saloon. As he explored the area wordlessly, he wore the expression of a house hunter who has, at last, found the perfect home.

From the cabin we went to the topside and started a tour of inspection which would have lasted the rest of the day, had not the Admiral been bound to go ashore and make his calls.

As he left the ship he told me that I should prepare for a reception he had planned to hold on the *Eagle*. All the cadets would be brought on board to act as hosts. The peo-ple of Hamilton would be invited by the Admiral and his staff. There would be a large crowd because he had visited Bermuda many times and had a wide circle of friends there.

It was apparent that our departure for the last leg of the trip could not take place until the cruise ship left. The Academy had scheduled a four day period for the cruise to remain there, so I resigned myself to this enforced holiday.

My American officers and I had friends among the officers of the cruise vessel, and this would have been a rare opportunity for a high old time, except that *we,* having been gone over six months and being anxious to get home to our families, found it tasteless. We were impatient to get going at the earliest moment.

Next day the Admiral took me along to lunch at the Governor General's house. The Governor General wanted to see the *Eagle* and was invited to come on board that afternoon. We returned to the ship ahead of the Governor's party and were at the gangway to receive him and render the proper honors as he came on board.

This time all hands were at general muster. As I looked around at the bronzed faces of the Americans and Germans, as I noted their proud bearing, it came to me that this trip had brought many benefits to each man on board. Every German had gained pounds—all muscle. They were a handsome lot. Many of the Americans had been fresh from farms and city streets just a few months ago. Now they looked every inch the sailormen they were.

This had been a remarkable trip in many ways. From the very beginning of the fitting out period in Bremerhaven until now, there had not been a single recorded case of misbehavior. The conduct book contained no entries. The appendicitis case and a couple of toothaches were the only occasions for medical treatment. No man had suffered an injury of any kind. The crew had remained completely free of venereal disease for the entire period. This is a record hard to equal.

After coffee in the cabin we went on the conducted tour that was now becoming such a familiar operation. The Admiral pointed to various features of the vessel with pride, and explained points of interest. He had missed very little in his brief inspection the day before. It was clear that he was as proud of the ship and her condition as we were.

178

The Governor General of Bermuda visits the *Eagle*.

We slatted about in a dead calm for the Admiral's benefit.

On the 4th of July my officers and I attended a big Independence Day party given by the American Consul General at his residence. The party was made additionally gay by the presence of a number of wives and friends of contestants in the bienniel Newport-to-Bermuda race. The race had started a few days before, but the lack of good sailing breezes had held up the arrival of the first of the racing craft. We of the Academy officers had a number of friends among the Bermuda racers and hoped they would start arriving before we had to leave. At the same time, I had been told by the harbor master that the arrival of this considerable number of yachts would make it necessary for me to move the *Eagle* away from her desirable anchorage. While I looked forward to seeing my friends, I did not want to lose my cozy berth.

While we were enjoying the Consul's party, our boy who had had the appendicitis attack at sea came down with a recurrence and was rushed to the Navy hospital, where a successful appendectomy was performed. From my point of view, this could not have happened at a better time. It seemed that everything was breaking my way. I was spared the necessity of deciding on an operation at sea, and was now free of the case. Come to think of it, all of our breaks had been good. Our busy little guardian angel had only a few more days' work to do. We were almost home.

The Academy reception made very little demand upon us of the *Eagle*. All we had to do was to hold still and be admired by the guests. The Admiral's staff and the cadet officers attended to the details. A few of the cadets were instructed in how to get about the vessel so that they could act as guides. We put on our best uniforms and awaited the beginning of the party, which was held in the early evening. Expectation of the number that would attend was far exceeded. They came in flocks, and seemed reluctant to leave. By mid-evening the ship was crowded and running boats

181

were busily engaged making continuous trips from the ship to the yacht club landing.

At the height of the party Ka-Leut came up to me and asked if the guests would like to hear his boys sing. Of course! He had assembled them on the fo'castle near the anchor windlass. Floating out of the darkness came the rich chords of classic German music. This singing had the disciplined stamp of training and was no haphazard, impromptu performance. As the music rose, a hush fell over the guests. I thought of a Sunday in the streets of Bremerhaven when I had paused before a German church and heard the same kind of music through the open door. The mood of the music changed, and the a cappella choir of virile male voices swung into gay songs of the sea. This unexpected bit of entertainment was the high point of the evening.

When the guests left the Admiral broke the news that he intended to sail with us next morning and watch us in action for the first few hours, at which time he would transfer to the flagship and we would go our separate ways. What a revolting development! The Admiral liked us *too* well! He was going to find out all about us, including our flaws, before this was over.

At first sign of light we got under way for the fuel dock, where we topped off our fuel and water tanks before taking on the Admiral. Fueling the *Eagle* is a simple operation because of her limited tank capacity. By mid-morning we were ready to sail, and without ceremony, steamed out the channel.

Here informal habits almost brought about a casualty. Although there was no breeze, the Admiral expressed a wish to see the sails set. Accordingly, the crew was sent aloft to start unfurling while we were still in the channel. The executive officer was conning the vessel with the assistance of the pilot, and I was standing off to one side discussing various features of the rigging with the Admiral.

When all gaskets had been removed from the furled sails on top of the yards, and this had been reported to the executive officer, he aimed his megaphone aloft and gave the command "Let fall!" whereupon the men on the yards released the sails and allowed them to drop into the clews. Upon hearing this command, the helmsman at the wheel mistook it for "Left full," which is not a proper order. (The correct command to a helmsman would have been: "Left full rudder.") Reflecting sketchy training in the niceties of accurate commands and responses, the helmsman mechanically repeated "Left full!" and started the wheel spinning to the left.

A sixth sense caused me to respond to the situation almost before I could think about it. Shoving the man away from the wheel, I spun it in the opposite direction in sufficient time to cause the ship to waver only slightly from her original course. To the left of the channel opposite us, bared teeth of newly cut coral grinned menacingly through the green crystal water, dangerously close. They would have bitten through the steel hull and brought our trip to an ignominious end within seconds.

With the situation again under control, I attempted to resume our conversation, although almost overcome by humiliation that this should have happened right before the Old Man's eyes. The Admiral mercifully appeared not to notice, and blandly steered the conversation to a new subject, giving me a chance to recover my composure. I resolved to give my line officers a bad time—subject: "Commands to the wheel and engine telegraphs."

The flagship followed us to a point well clear of Bermuda. The intention was to photograph the *Eagle* from all angles with all sails set but the weather was unaccommodating. What hint of a breeze there had been in the early morning died away, leaving us in a completely dead calm. I wanted to abandon the project, but the Admiral's eager-

183

ness to see everything set was so keen that he insisted we go ahead in the hope that some breeze might spring up.

One by one we set all the sails—and lay there dead in the water, slatting about in the swell made by the flagship as it steamed back and forth relentlessly photographing us in our shame. The sails hung like flour sacks; blocks clattered against the standing rigging.

After a couple of hours of this the Admiral finally gave the welcome word that we could go on our way, and he reluctantly transshipped and headed south. We set to the job of furling, and had our engine going in short order . Toward evening we sighted a few of the belated Bermuda racers who were also trapped on the polished surface of the windless sea.

The excitement of having the Admiral on board and the attendant activity had not given me an opportunity to tell Doc the good news about the appendicitis case. Word from the hospital was that the operation had been normal and a quick recovery could be expected. When I broke the news to Doc, he put on a creditable bit of histrionics, pretending to fall into a mood of black despair over missing out on the operation. I will never know whether or not he was serious. By the time for evening star sights he had resumed his role as assistant navigator, and was busily at work in the chart house plotting our position.

Just before sunset a refreshing southeast breeze came sweeping in, heralding its approach with a dark line marking the ruffled surface from horizon to horizon. As the welcome switch in weather reached us, we set lower courses and tops'ls and settled down for another night at sea, happy in the prospect that only a few hours separated us from the end of our trip.

Chapter XIII

As darkness approached, I felt a small twinge of uneasiness—a vague wordless worry that I could not identify. I was overlooking something important.

Could it be that I had sailed from Bermuda leaving something undone? I scratched around in my mental work locker looking for the cause. I have occasionally been guilty of disorderly and impulsive thinking, but this time I was certain that everything was shipshape. Our tanks were full, we had sufficient stores, I had received the necessary permission to leave the port; none of the crew was missing except the man in the hospital; this was too late in the day for a hangover. As I paced the quarterdeck I searched through my mind, probing here and there, much as a navigator sweeps the horizon ahead looking for his first evidence of land.

Pacing aft, I stopped and ran my eyes over the rigging aloft. The ship was neat and taut, no Irish pennants, no yards cockbilled; apple pie order. I looked skyward. A thin veil of cirrus was dimming the stars. Before this they had been abnormally bright. All of a sudden it came to me. Something about the weather was simply not right.

A check showed that the barometer was behaving in a peculiar fashion. The characteristic daily undulation of barometric pressure which is common to the tropical and sub-tropical part of the world in normal weather was missing, and had been for ten hours. Two easy weeks in the northeast trades had spoiled me. At any other time I would have checked the barograph record as a matter of habit every time I passed it.

The barograph is a lazy man's way of keeping track of the barometric changes which take place. This little machine consists of a vertical cylinder about four inches high and two inches in diameter, upon which is fastened a new paper chart every twenty-four hours. The cylinder revolves by clockwork and is, in fact, a type of clock. The paper record has curving lines from top to bottom marking the hours and minutes. Running horizontally along the record are parallel lines calibrated in hundredths of an inch. An inking stylus which is operated by an aneroid barometer tracks upward and downward, tracing the behavior of the barometric pressure and recording the changes, hour by hour, as the day goes by. The semi-diurnal variation of the barometer in tropical areas of the world is simply a rising and falling of barometric pressure, much like tidal action which occurs twice in each twenty-four hour period, the high part of the curve occurring at about 10 A.M. and 10 P.M. local time, and the low occurring about 4 A.M. and 4 P.M.

This behavior continues day after day and week after week in fair, uneventful weather. The deeper into the tropics a ship proceeds, the more pronounced is this hill-and-dale action. As you reach higher latitudes the action grows fainter, until at about the latitude of New York it becomes barely noticeable. It is axiomatic that the words frequently seen on the faces of aneroid barometers—"Fair," "Change," "Storm," mean practically nothing. What is important is the trend. A glance at the curve on the barograph recording sheet tells you what you need to know. When I looked, the pressure recording was almost a straight horizontal line on the cylinder.

I studied the sky and convinced myself that bad weather signs were there for the reading. Could an undetected tropical disturbance lie at the base of the faintly

186

outlined fan-like cirrus formation I remembered seeing in the west just before sunset? Probably.

I sent for the Exec.

"How's the weather look to you?"

"All right, Cap'n. If this breeze holds we ought to make New York day after tomorrow morning."

"I hope you're right, but somehow I feel there is something fishy going on."

My Exec was a young man who had been plunged into the war shortly after graduation from the Academy, and moved from one position of responsibility to another. At war's end he was in command of a destroyer escort. By the leisurely standards of the pre-war years, he would just now be graduating to the exalted position of senior watch officer, three steps down from a command position. In spite of his short service he had matured rapidly and, as a competent seaman, had my full confidence. He had had a lot of experience, but he had had it in a hurry.

"I can't put my finger on it precisely, but I have the feeling we're going to get a dusting between here and New York."

"Well, Cap'n, by now my gang can work together pretty smoothly. I think we should be able to handle any squall situation between here and home."

"I don't know. That sunset tonight reminded me of some I've seen just before real bad weather. Has the radio man been copying the weather today?"

"Come to think of it, Cap'n, I don't believe he has. With the Admiral on board and all the excitement that's been going on ever since dawn, I think I saw the radio man a time or two heaving on a line."

"Where's the radio file?"

We checked through it. There were occasional entries up to the day before sailing. What weather entries there were appeared to indicate normal summer conditions.

187

There was one disturbing little notation to the effect that the receiver had been behaving in an in-and-out manner. It was possible that some vital weather broadcast had been missed.

"Look here, young fellow, let's review the recent hours. I get the distinct feeling that I've been seeing signs and paying no attention to them. The sunset, for example. Weathermen say that a fanlike cirrus formation accompanies bad weather, but I've often seen the same thing when it was blue bird weather for a thousand miles. That barograph has lost its semi-diurnal variation. You can add it all up and get pessimistic over the future. I have a feeling it would be wise to change course right now and head due west. If there is anything lumpy in that direction, it should move up to the northeastward and we would move in behind it."

"Gee whiz, Cap'n, we've been such a long time gone from home our wives have probably forgotten us by now. Anyway, I, for one, want to get home. Cap'n, if there was anything really big over there we were bound to have picked it up in Bermuda. I haven't heard a word about anything out of the ordinary."

"The truth is, neither have I. Maybe I'm just trying to argue myself into bad weather."

Feeling that I had been acting like a silly old woman and reading weather signs that were enhanced by an apprehensive imagination, I decided not to alter the course.

It is the duty of the navigator (in this case, my executive officer) to advise the captain on matters pertaining to the ship's course and position and possible dangers, but here his responsibility ends. If the captain makes the right decision, it is only what is expected of him. If he guesses wrong, he must make the best of it, hoping experience and knowledge can recover the situation, and that whatever misadventures he and the ship have will be minimized to the

point of going unnoticed. Something buried in my sub-
conscious—something akin to instinct—suggested that I was
making the wrong move, but I followed Napoleon's rule—
"Order, counter-order, disorder," and let matters stand.

The gentle breeze freshened somewhat and then held
steady. Coming from the southeast, it carried us merrily
along toward home. After everything had been snugged
down for sea I continued to pace the quarterdeck. The
barometer held steady. By midnight I decided to turn in.
Taking a last look around, I noticed that the overlay of
cirrus had thickened and that the stars were barely visible.
The breeze and the barometer continued reassuringly without change, so I went to the sea cabin. Not feeling especially sleepy, I lay down for the rest.

Suddenly I was wide awake. It was still dark. I became
aware of sound—W I N D! The soft monotone of the steady
breeze was gone. A gusty, uneven moaning had taken its
place. The ship was lurching in an uneasy fashion as
though in a resentful mood. I hurried outside to have a
look.

The air felt wet and sticky. I groped forward through
the dense humid darkness to the steering station, where the
OD and helmsmen were silhouetted by the pale yellow radi-
ance from the binnacle. The green haze fanning out from
the starboard side-light was an indication that the air was
almost completely saturated with moisture. The temperature had risen, and the burbling wind, which the evening
before had been a cool pleasant companion, was now the
fetid breath of bad weather.

The OD greeted me with a nervous smile.

"How long has this been going on?"

"It just started, Cap'n."

The wind was coming in irregular gusts. A check of the
anemometer showed that the force was moderate. My
thoughts turned to the previous day, and for the first time

189

I remembered the long, oily slick swell of the afternoon before when we had been slatting around with all sails set. In all textbooks on tropical storms this omen is listed among the earliest indications of an approaching disturbance.

The long low swells which sometimes announce tropical storms have been observed as much as two or three days ahead of the bad weather. They are most likely to make themselves felt in areas of otherwise undisturbed waters, with calm air such as we had had yesterday. Some years before, on ice patrol duty near the Grand Banks of Newfoundland, I had seen an excellent example of this weather omen. In my innocence of weather knowledge, I had admired the gentle sine-curve shaped horizon, the orderly rows of wave tops rolling majestically along the skyline from southwest to northeast. Under the abnormal visibility conditions, the horizon had been sharp as the serrated cutting edge of a bread knife. Two days later we had a mountainous sea and the wind came near blowing the masts out of the vessel.

In the gray of coming light I took an anxious look at the low flying clouds scudding in from the eastward. Short showers of fine rain swept over us periodically. At first they were barely noticeable, more like spray or mist than rain. By dawn the barograph announced the bad news. The needle was plunging downward. We were in for a blow.

Good light was slow in coming. As the clock indicated sunrise, the thickening overcast absorbed the growing light, leaving us in a pre-dawn gloom. Spitting rain squalls gradually increased in frequency and intensity. The squally puffs of breeze, each a little stronger than the last, began to veer, hauling and backing as much as two full points. In the growing suspicion that I had a real hurricane on my hands, I made a careful estimate of the situation.

As specified in the night orders of the previous evening, we had the upper and lower foretops'ls, the upper and

190

lower main tops'ls, and the fores'l and mains'l set and showing no signs of strain. Should I leave them set or play it
safe? These sails are of the heaviest canvas we used and
could be expected to stand a lot of wind. But—how much
wind were we likely to get?

Using the seaman's estimate of the direction the center
of the storm lay, I faced the wind, mentally pointing my
right hand toward the horizon ninety degrees to the right.
If we were in the system of a tropical hurricane, the storm
center should lie about in the direction I was pointing. In
our latitude, which was roughly half way between Bermuda
and New York, a tropical storm should have already re-
curved, and should be heading in a northeasterly direction.
By this time the mean direction of the ever increasing puffs
and squalls was northeasterly. If my estimate was correct,
the storm center should be southeast of us and should pass
clear upon its northeasterly course.

Another possibility was that we were in an isolated squall
area that was not yet giving a true indication of the location
of the storm, nor its direction of travel. If this were true,
the conservative thing would be to get some of the sail off
in order to be more manageable later on. Somewhere I had
read that the most successful skippers of square-riggers were
those who dared to drive a ship, and that many times the
safety of a vessel, paradoxically, lay in the skipper's daring
to keep sail on when conservatism dictated that it should
come off. I chose to keep what sail I had set and run before
the weather, bearing to the westward as much as possible,
trusting this would haul us clear of the center. To this day
I don't know what, if any, bearing my bold decision had on
events which followed.

I relieved the OD and proceeded to con the ship myself.

The eight-to-noon watch came on. The executive officer
was busily directing the details of storm preparations. He
was grateful for the use of the extra officer on the deck work,

191

as I took the watch. All hands were engaged in putting extra lashings on the boats, rigging lifelines, securing airports, dogging down hatches and closing watertight doors. By mid-morning everything was as secure as we could make it.

Now I was no longer in doubt about the outcome of the weather. The mounting crescendo of the wind, the thickening rain squalls, the rapidly building sea and the nose-diving barograph were my informants. If this were a well-shaped, proper type of hurricane following traditional patterns of behavior, we should run through the westerly edge of it with no more than a moderate dusting.

Running before the weather, as we were doing, we no longer steered a course. Our heading was determined by the wind direction alone. I resolved to keep the wind nearly astern, favoring starboard over port. As long as the wind stayed northeast it would take us in toward the New Jersey coast, and, I hoped, out of the system of this devilish weather. Frequent glances at the compass were for the purpose of keeping informed about where the wind was taking us. Until we could get a sight of sun or stars, our navigation would be strictly guesswork, but I was doing a little dead reckoning of sorts as we went along.

Up until the time the sea began to build to impressive size, we went boiling along, taking full advantage of the wind without being tossed about. Good! Every mile behind us shortened the time we would be in this mess, if my estimate was correct and the disturbance was moving northeastward.

Soon after I took over the conning job, the two helmsmen began to lag. It was customary for the man on the left side of the wheel to act as the leading helmsman, and his movements would be followed and assisted by his teammate on the opposite spokes. I turned impatiently to the lead

It begins to blow.

The *Eagle* in Hurricane Carol.

helmsman, on the point of snapping a demand for smarter steering, but stopped when I saw his expression.

"What's the matter, man? Are you having trouble?"

"Yes, sir. The wheel is fighting back."

Looking aft I saw the reason for his trouble. In the rising sea the swells were beginning to overtake us, each crest coming in from a slightly different angle, and delivering a wallop to the underside of our old-fashioned overhanging counter. This shock was feeding through the steering mechanism with such force that it threatened to throw the helmsmen off their feet. The next time the Exec came bustling by, I halted him.

"This job is getting too big for two men. Let's have two more."

With four men working as a team, things went smoothly for a little while. As the weather developed our steering load increased, and we piled on more hands until eight men were gathered around toiling at the spokes. When I first saw this rig I had been curious about the need for the multiple positions for what, in my naïveté, appeared to be a simple job. I was now learning the hard way why the Germans had been so generous in preparing for exactly this situation, and was grateful for the stout two-inch steel drive-shaft which led from the wheel to the rudder.

As the wind fishtailed angrily about us, I was constantly snapping orders at the helmsmen, while I kept my neck craned aloft to gauge its direction by the commission pennant flying from the main truck. My helmsmen and I were a tight little island of humanity on the broad quarterdeck. Others were moving back and forth along the lifelines, but the intensity of our concentration on our task welded us into a single unit detached from the goings-on around us.

I had been busily engaged for about five hours, but excitement pumped a lot of adrenalin and I felt no weariness.

195

There had been no morning coffee and no breakfast but I gave this not a thought. A strange feeling of elation gripped me as I watched the drama unfold. I was living in the moment and time was standing still. If the quartermaster was marking the passage of time with the ship's bell, it was a futile gesture, since the ding-dinging would not have registered on our consciousness.

Whitecaps had long since disappeared and been replaced by angry streaks gouged on the breast of the waves by the claws of the wind. Puffs became roaring blasts of wind. The average velocity rose above fifty knots. This brought another change in the sea. The streaks on the surface vanished, giving way to clouds of spray as wavetops were sheared off by the wind.

When this occurs there comes a momentary period of deceptive smoothness. The stinging pellets of water fly horizontally downwind, knocking down the waves as they try to rise. It gives a false sense of calm, but experience tells the seaman that this will quickly pass. At this point a really big sea begins building. From here on the storm will approach maturity. If it has previously crossed open ocean, the waves will already be huge and the violence of the wind will be building them larger. But if the storm has recently passed across land, the building of a sea of dangerous size takes a long time.

The spitting showers merged into dense heavy rain. As I strained my eyes aloft toward the barely visible commission pennant, I could feel the sting as the large drops bit into the back of my neck and hammered upon my shoulder blades.

I had weathered hurricanes before, but never in this manner. All the ships I had served in heretofore had had snug, closed bridges. At best, getting through a hurricane is a rugged, uncomfortable experience. This business of being out in the open and taking what Nature dishes out is a test of endurance. With no sign of a slackening in the barometer drop, I was fully aware that this was only the beginning, and as awesome as the weather looked, it was bound to get worse.

Chapter XIV

The job of conning while we ran before it grew more demanding as the wind rapidly shifted direction, and my rudder commands swerved the ship from side to side, following the whims of the blasting air. A big sea began to build. Another couple of hours of this and it would be mountainous. As the sea rose, there appeared to be eight or ten ship lengths from crest to crest.

One would think that each sea should be successively larger than the one that comes before it, but this is not true. We might expect uniformity if the wind behaved in a neat, orderly fashion and blew in a straight line. A hurricane is roughly circular in shape, with the winds spiralling in toward the center in a counter-clockwise direction in the northern hemisphere. This brings about a constantly changing direction of force on the surface of the water, and is further complicated by the storm's never being truly circular, having endless local variations throughout its area.

Occasionally a storm center may break into two or more whirling "eyes," which may come back together or wander apart, each in its own crazy fashion. In the eye of the storm there is a momentary calm so far as the wind is concerned, but in which confused seas rush haphazardly in from all directions; where colliding wave fronts explode skyward, and where no ship can choose a comfortable safe heading. This is why mariners attempt to avoid the eye at all costs.

Although the wave lengths appeared to be fairly constant, the size of each wave gave no inkling of what to expect next. Sailormen have various theories about the nature of mountainous seas. How often I have heard it said that every seventh wave is a humdinger, and among these periodic "sevenths" there comes an occasional "daddy of them all."

With the beginning of the big seas the wind velocity rose sharply. A messenger checked the anemometer indicatoı and barograph inside the chart house at regular intervals. Each time he returned he brought bad news. The wind average by now was about sixty knots, and the barometric pressure was still going down. This repetition of ill tidings grew irksome.

As the ship began to plunge and wallow when each crest overtook us and went roaring by, it became hard to retain a footing, with the increasing blasts of wind at our backs. All hands were directed to remain where they were until further notice, and there would be no relieving of watches except for the relays of eight men at a time on the wheel. Even with this large number of willing hands straining to control the crazy thing, they tired rapidly and had to be relieved at from fifteen to twenty minute intervals. The pool of manpower for the task was clustered about the quarterdeck, hanging on to life lines and railings.

I found that I could manage very nicely by wedging myself between the binnacle and the engine telegraph. This station is just forward and very close to the steering station, and I directed my team from here with the use of hand signals, indicating by a gesture whether the wheel should go to the right or to the left. By now, shouted commands could no longer be understood for the noise of the wind.

The tonal range of wind sound is almost unbelievable. The earlier skirling and piping of the fresh gale through the rigging had risen in volume and in tone to bellowing and shrieking. The vast sound seemed to fill the world. Voices of men died away and became inaudible. Each man finds himself suddenly alone with the wind. Lips moving, neck cords and veins standing out recalled the silent movie days. Here were faces transmitting thoughts by expression

199

alone. Here was sound without sound. It pressed upon eardrums and bodies as a solid thing. The singleness of this mighty roar brought about a solitude. The weight of wind and sound tightened our isolated worlds about us.

The massiveness of the sea, dwarfing the ship, in proportion created the illusion of slow motion. The illusion was shattered into hard reality as we dove into each trough and felt the shock of the solid wall of water. As each wave front approached from astern, the advancing face of the wave seemed to steepen and bear down upon us with a rolling motion that is seen in miniature when breakers curl in on a beach. The mares' tails of flying spume streaming from each crest were horizontal cascades, merging with the pounding rain, completing the optical illusion.

Each time we were overtaken our stern rose high in the air. As the wave moved forward the stern would begin to settle on the back of the wave, and momentarily the ship would be suspended at her midship point with bow and stern protruding, each from its own side of the watery ridge. At this moment tons of water plunged in from port and starboard, filling the welldeck. Here another feature of the *Eagle's* design was revealed. My lonely little colony on the quarterdeck was not being swept by green water—small comfort in view of the punishment being absorbed, but one thing less to worry about at this moment.

The voice of the storm was more than a roar. There was the sharp tearing sound—the ripping of the fabric of the gates of hell. The bellowing blasts, born of the heat of the tropics, slowly accumulated during months of gestation at the edge of the Doldrums, were the main theme. This tapestry of sound bore the pattern of maniacal majesty.

The fore upper and lower tops'ls were the first to go. One moment they were there; a second later they had vanished. It seemed incredible that all that remained of the broad spread of sail were these ragged little ribbons. Where

200

had the canvas gone? Was it possible that these remnants could have made up the whole sail?

I looked at the revolution counter which was geared to the propeller shaft. While the vessel was under sail the propeller was disengaged by the clutch and allowed to turn free, and as the ship moved through the water the screw action caused it to revolve. We had learned through experience that our free turning propeller was a reliable log and indicated the speed at a ratio of ten to one; that at 80 rpm on the free turning screw we would be logging exactly eight knots. The needle stood steady at 160 rpm. Sixteen knots! Ka-Leut had told me that the fastest the *Horst Wessel* had ever sailed had been fourteen.

While I was engaged in this useless speed estimate, the fores'l and main upper tops'l blew out. The mains'l and main lower tops'l still held. Our speed slackened, but only slightly.

I felt a tug at my sleeve, and looked up to find the Danish passenger trying to get my attention. With his twenty-five years' experience in square-riggers, I expected to find nonchalance and quiet confidence in his manner, but instead there was fear in his eyes. Up to that moment, my exhilaration, born of excitement and intense concentration on my task, had left no room for self doubts. I felt a wave of impatience at his interruption. He shouted into my ear. A tiny voice came through as from a great distance:

"Cap-tain, don't you t'ink maybe pretty soon ve heave to?"

I nodded and shaped the word, "Soon," but turned my attention back to the demanding job of conning. I glanced astern. The advancing face of each wave was almost vertical. By now the mountainous sea was well developed. Along the top of every giant wave was a smother of foam, from which spewed a Niagara of spray as it was torn away and swept downwind.

The mixture of spray and rain searched out every tiny opening in our clothing. The only protection the foul weather gear afforded was against the sting of the liquid buckshot coming from sky and sea. A messenger brought word that the anemometer needle was at the top of the scale. The wind velocity was beyond eighty knots!

Each passing moment brought the conviction that now this storm was as bad as it could possibly get. When the seas have become mountainous and the wind has gone beyond seventy-five knots, the senses are deceived. Finally a kind of bemused wonder, no longer questioning, pervades the mind.

Occasional glances at the compass revealed that the general direction of the wind had backed from northeast to north. This meant that the center of the storm, if it behaved itself, should move clear of us, but brought little comfort in the face of the ever-increasing wind and sea, and a continuing devilish falling of the barograph.

I turned to the idea of heaving to. The ship had begun to dive and wallow like a wounded wild thing. Each time a wave overtook us I looked apprehensively astern. As the stern began to lift on the face of a wave, the bowsprit dipped deeper and deeper until it disappeared from sight. When each crest swept from aft forward, the stern settled deeply upon the back of the wave, and the bowsprit pointed toward the sky. The water that had been scooped up by the fo'cas'le would come thundering aft, burying everything in the welldeck under a foamy green burden. As the *Eagle* shook herself like a giant dog, tons of water tore out through the freeing ports. I began to count the seas, looking for the mighty "Seventh."

Mentally I reviewed the business of heaving to. There are various methods used on power vessels, but there is not much choice under sail. The ship must be in a position where she will ride most easily in relation to the sea and

202

wind. Once this position is assumed, the ultimate outcome is out of the hands of her skipper, and will be decided by fate and the ship's designers. When the ship is hove to, the captain and crew become observers.

There is much difference of opinion among professional seamen about the best method of heaving to on a ship under power. The term "heave to" comes to us from the days of sail and literally means "to stop." Modern passenger giants rarely heave to because their size and power give them a big advantage over most weather. The accepted idea of heaving to is the abandoning of the course which takes you toward your destination, and placing the ship at an angle to the wind and sea best devised to protect the ship and passengers from injury. Some skippers head a steamship almost into the wind and keep the engines barely turning, with just enough headway to make steering possible.

In recent years some hardy souls have reasoned that a ship would suffer less damage by going away from the wind, and, at the risk of being "pooped," have steamed slowly downwind. Being pooped means having a sea break over the stern and sweep forward across the poop deck, tearing away everything exposed to the destructive hydraulic ram of power. In either event, heaving to on a steamer calls for continuing effort on the part of the captain and crew in fighting with wheel and engines, to keep the ship at a proper angle to the sea. A sailing vessel abandons all pretense of struggle, and literally rolls with the punches.

Each look astern made me dread this moment of decision. To reach the hove to position the ship would have to be turned through an angle of more than ninety degrees in order to have the wind and seas coming in from slightly forward of the beam. This moment of turning presents grave danger of broaching and having the ship go over on her beam ends. If the *Eagle* broached, it would be the end of us all.

A messenger crawled hand over hand along the lifeline from the radio shack, and delivered a crumpled wet dispatch from an American freighter:

"URGENT TO ALL SHIPS AM IN LATITUDE 37-30 N LONGITUDE 72-30 W UNABLE TO MANEUVER IN HEAVY WIND AND SEA ALL VESSELS THIS VICINITY PLEASE KEEP CLEAR MASTER"

The operator had scribbled at the bottom of the message: "Loud signal—sounds close."

"Poor devil," I thought. That skipper must have sent his message out to bolster his own morale. It could not serve any other purpose. Our visibility was only a few yards. If he should suddenly loom up out of the murk ahead, there would not be a chance in the world of avoiding a collision. We would both be dead ducks.

I thought for a moment about the futility of abandoning ship in this sea if the worst should happen. It would be impossible. No small boat could live, even if it should be lucky enough to get away from the ship's side without being dashed to pieces. Ours was a case of being utterly committed to the job of hanging on right where we were and making the best of it.

My next visitor was the Exec, who indicated through sign language that he wanted to know my decision about heaving to. Moments before he asked, something had happened which removed all doubt from my mind about our course of action. Along came a sea that was the daddy of them all, and caught us at a slight angle, the very thing I had been trying to avoid. The ship partially broached, and with a thunderous "Bang!" literally dove into the ocean. The bowsprit and entire fo'cas'le disappeared under green water

204

all the way to the base of the forem'st. The mains'l exploded like a child's balloon. We rolled deeply to starboard. We hung momentarily at the bottom of the roll, while I stared across the quarterdeck, looking almost straight down at the boiling surface of the ocean. My ship quivered—and fought her way upright with laboring effort. We couldn't take many repetitions of this.

At this point I had a strange mental reaction. For a moment I imagined myself a detached spectator. I seemed to be two people discussing the wild scene. I remember saying: "This is a hell of a situation. I have come over 5000 miles and now it is possible that I could lose this ship." I looked around at the crew with a keen sense of sorrow that these husky young men should be wasted in this fruitless effort. I cursed myself for not having followed what I had considered an impulse the night before when I had failed to change course to westward. At that moment it did not occur to me that if the ship went down I would go along.

The time to heave to was *right now*. We rehearsed the maneuver in pantomime and agreed that the Exec would give me a wave of the hand when his boys were ready to haul at the braces. I whistled the engine room, ordered the shaft connected, and told them to stand by the engine telegraph for a short "ahead" bell.

When the Exec indicated that he was ready to go into action, I watched the advancing seas, waiting for the most favorable moment to start my swing to port. We had agreed that we would heave to on the port tack with our remaining main lower tops'l still set, provided the wind didn't blow it away. At the same time, we would set the small lower mizzens'l in order to strike a balance with the forward sail.

An example of broaching can be seen when a rider on a surf board loses control and instead of shooting along on the fore part of a wave, skids off to one side and slams into the sea as his board snaps around in a ninety degree turn. I had had only one bit of initiation in a near broach, and this had been on a destroyer back in the 1920's. We had been cruising along at a moderate speed near Pt. Judith, Rhode Island, running before a fairly large sea. In the execution of a previously ordered change of course, I had blithely put my rudder over just *before* a rather big wave overtook our stern. The next thing that happened broke all the dishes in the wardroom. The destroyer whipped over almost on its side and skidded around in a half circle, in a matter of seconds. Only a watchful guardian angel had prevented us from losing men overboard. Now I was thankful for that impromptu rehearsal. This time the turn would be made on the back, and not the front of the wave.

Immediately after the next and largest wave bore down upon us and swept by with the ship on a fairly normal angle to the sea, I gave the Exec a wave of the hand, and ordered my toiling helmsmen to put the wheel over to left full rudder, at the same time ringing ahead two-thirds on the engine telegraph. As the ship's head began to swing, I stopped the engine and began to pray. The next thirty seconds would be critical.

The boys on the braces and those on the mizzens'l sensed our dangerous situation. They worked with desperate haste. The ship snapped around to her new heading as though mounted on a pivot; the yards were braced around, lines set taut. The mizzens'l zipped into place. It was as though the whole operation had been performed by one pair of giant hands. When the next sea came along, we were ready for it.

With the combination of sails and rudder angle we would now find out how well the *Eagle* could take care of herself. The arrangement of the ballast was all important. If the ship were too stiff and had a tendency to ride upright without enough "give" we would take a worse beating than

206

before. If she were too tender, a continuing increase in wind and sea, and we would finally go over.

As the first sea bore down upon us, the towering cliff face of water appeared higher than our masts. It seemed impossible that our little craft could survive the climb up this precipice—"little craft," because at that moment she did seem little—an example of changing values.

Glancing quickly forward and aft, I caught fleeting glimpses of the crew bringing order out of the apparent chaos of loose lines after the yards had been braced around. The mass of loose line that accumulates behind a man who is hauling on a purchase looks like a hopeless tangle, and can become so if it is not promptly put in order. There was no confusion here. The line was being swiftly gathered, coiled and stopped, ready for use again when needed. My trusty Exec had not made an idle boast when he supposed that his crowd could handle themselves in squally weather. Right now the sea was testing them and they looked good under the stress.

As we started our roller-coaster rise, I could feel the steadying influence the wind was exerting on our sail and rigging. It was as if a huge hand were lifting the vessel gently up and over the crest. Being accustomed to the wild gyrations of power vessels under similar circumstances, I was surprised and delighted at the gentle lowering into the next trough. The ship was as steady as a church. It was like a ride on a well controlled elevator. Under the pressure of the wind, we were heeled to starboard at about a twenty-degree angle, but the wild confusion was over. As the sails began to draw at their sharp angle to the wind, forward movement of the vessel caused her to feel her rudder and head slightly more to windward. With this change in direction, the sails began to spill, thus losing headway and cancelling the rudder action. As the bow fell off slightly,

207

the sails again began to draw. This cycle occurred about every five minutes.

While I was enjoying the relief from the recent strain and struggle, I noticed our number one bosun's mate—the same lad who had exhibited his skill with the bosun's pipe in Madeira and Bermuda—hustling aft with the sure-footed stride of a born sailorman. His lips were moving—the son-of-a-gun was singing at the top of his voice! He had been doing this all through the storm, seemingly having the time of his life. Even though his song was being snatched away by the wind, the sight of him gave my spirits a lift.

After watching our progress for a while, it was clear to me that we could weather comfortably a whole lot more than we were getting now. There was no conning to do with the wheel lashed in the full left position. I called for an OD to relieve me, and popped into the chart house.

The clock on the bulkhead struck four bells in the afternoon watch. There stood Doc, literally bug-eyed with excitement. I grabbed a towel and was drying my face and hands, anticipating my first cigarette of the day. I tried to light up and found my fingers so shriveled I could not handle a match. I asked Doc to light one for me.

"Gosh, Cap'n," a quivering finger pointed at the anemometer; "Do you know what the wind's been doing? It's been blowing over a hundred miles an hour!"

"I know, Doc, I know. Just light that cigarette. Where do you think I've been for the past eight hours?"

My words were ignored.

"Look at that barograph; that needle's been going almost straight down!"

While Doc was talking I noted that the wind velocity had not abated. By comparison, our new heading made both wind and sea seem far less fearsome. My growing assurance was strengthened by a look at the barograph.

The needle was leveling off. The blow was not over, but this was an encouraging sign.

The buildup of a storm at sea carries with it a conditioning effect upon the men on a ship. One's senses absorb the experience of sound, motion, the impact of air and water, the wild ride the body gets as the ship reels and staggers. All of these grow familiar and can achieve a sort of monotony through repetition. A motorist on a smooth highway gradually becomes accustomed to high speed, and is frequently surprised when he looks down at the speedometer and sees 80 or even 90 miles an hour indicated by the arrow. When forced to slow down, he finds moderate speed a snail's pace by comparison. In the past eight hours we had reached the point where we now looked upon a wild sea and listening to hurricane winds with a fair amount of equanimity. The leveling off of the barograph, with just a faint hint of an upturn, meant far more to me than a mere ink tracing on a paper cylinder. It was not a smooth tracing, but had a jagged feathery edge imposed by the excessive motion of the vessel.

This was the first hint of victory. The barometer must rise as the storm center drew away from us, and the fact that the wind had backed a full 90 degrees meant that the storm center had traveled in the direction I hoped it would when I made my original estimate of the situation. The principal thing wrong with that estimate was that the center came a hell of a lot closer to us than I had wanted it to, and that we had gotten, and were still getting, something more than a brisk dusting. As I watched the barograph line, I had a feeling of downright affection for the little machine, and resisted the impulse to give it a friendly pat.

Doc continued his lecture about how awesome the storm had been and still was, as though I had just come on board and needed bringing up to date. I got a kick out of his

209

ranting. He seemed proud of having witnessed such a terrific show. He had stuck at his post, following the progress of the storm, his excitement mounting every minute. Our anemometer registered in meters per second, and by means of a conversion table mounted on the bulkhead, he had been busily translating to nautical miles per hour every few minutes. He gave me a running account of his observations.

My Danish passenger came in to mop off and have a smoke. He had been helping with the mizzens'l. He wore a broad grin.

"By gosh, Cap-tain, I vas scar't as hell back dere before ve heave to. Now everyt'ing iss fine."

"What were you afraid of?"

"Vell, I don't know about ballast; I don't know about dis rig—"

"Maybe you don't know about this skipper, either, huh?"

"Oh, you do all right, Cap-tain. It is yust dis new ship and de vorst blow I ever see."

"Vorst blow I ever see too. I hope everybody fared all right."

It then occurred to me that we had a poor devil locked in the brig. He had been a last minute transfer from the cruise ship when we left Bermuda, and was to be delivered to New London for court-martial. Whatever his offense, it had been committed before the two ships met in Hamilton harbor. I doubted whether he had been fed in all the excitement. What must have been his sensations in his steel barred solitude, with all hell breaking loose outside and nary a soul coming near him!

Ka-Leut came in. Taking his extended hand in some puzzlement, I wondered what was on his mind.

"Cap-tain, you are one fine seaman."

I felt a mixture of pleasure and keen embarrassment.

210

"You were brave to run before it so long. It was perhaps this that took us clear of the center of the storm."

I was glad he could not read my mind. What had just happened had been thrust upon me. I felt like a sparrow that had been caught in a badminton game. We were badly mussed, but we were still afloat and in fair shape.

By three in the afternoon the barograph showed a positive upward trend. The pressure was rising almost as fast as it had fallen. This, together with a gradual wind shift to the northwest told me that the storm was dying. Rather suddenly, the wind dropped below sixty knots. From here on our recovery was rapid.

I went on deck to inspect the damage.

Chapter XV

In just a few moments $20,000 worth of sails had gone with the wind. Could they have been saved? Yes, but to do so would have been the result of a better estimate of the situation in the beginning, or, later, at great risk to life and limb.

In the first case, I had committed myself and could not turn back time. In the second case, I would not, under any circumstances, allow any man to try to furl or reef after the storm was upon us. As it was, fate had been good. The record of no injuries remained unblemished. I felt no regrets.

As I turned from examining the rigging, I noticed that a man standing nearby was red-faced and appeared feverish.

"What's the matter with you, boy? You look like a boiled lobster."

"I'm O.K., Cap'n. Your face is red too. So is everybody else's."

I looked around and found that it was so. The stinging of the wind and spray had burned and bruised our skins. At a glance you could tell who had been out in the weather and who had been safely behind watertight doors during the blow.

The tattered remains of the sails gave the ship a raffish air. We were eager to go about the job of bending on fresh sails, but must wait for further abatement of the weather. Although conditions were improving from minute to minute, and conversations could be resumed by dint of shouting, there was still a fifty-knot breeze and a dangerous sea.

Without being told to do so, one of the German petty

After the storm, the Skipper (center) surveys the damage.

Things are returning to normal but the life lines are still in place.

officers went scrambling up the fore ratlines, intent upon getting away some of the debris, impatient to begin putting OUR ship in order.

"Get our man down, Herr Ka-Leut! We've been lucky so far. We can't gamble now."

A messenger was sent to retrieve our enthusiastic volunteer.

During the idyllic balmy days of our passage from Madeira to Bermuda I had day-dreamed, picturing our triumphal entry into New York harbor. I had hoped for a spanking southerly breeze which would enable us to go bowling up the channel with everything set, with sun-bleached white sails against a bright summer sky, brass and bright work reflecting the brilliant morning sunlight, and immaculate white paint work accented by contrasting spar color. We would round up smartly opposite Quarantine, down would go the anchor, and nary a puff from our shameful engine exhaust would foul the fresh morning air. The natives ashore would gape with awe and admiration as the husky lads swarmed aloft to do a neat man-o-war furling job.

Although this dream, full of vanity, was gone, I felt a surge of satisfaction with the ship and crew. Our initiation had been a severe one. Those of us new to square-riggers had taken our first test in the highest order of seamanship and were still on our feet. As I watched my huskies putting the ship in order, I had my proof that a square-rigged sailing ship is a good place for a greenhorn to get his introduction to the sea.

By sunset the sky had cleared. The storm was over. The sea had gone down, and before dark we resumed our journey.

Tomorrow we would be home.

214

Afterword

28 June 1996, Hamburg, Germany:

The lyrical strains of "Shenandoah" drift across the deck of *Eagle*, a surreal blend of the heavily-accented male voices of the German chantey choir with the youthful male and female cadets of the United States Coast Guard Academy. *Could the Skipper have imagined . . . ?*

The crowd on deck is a curious mixture of about 70 elderly Germans, all former *Horst Wessel* crew members, aged about 65 to 75 years, socializing with the youth of *Eagle*. These Germans stand a little taller and the look of youth is in their eyes as they walk the decks of their former ship, but I can't help detecting a sense of sadness as if many of them realize that this may be the last visit in their lifetime. Some of them served with Ka-Leut at the end of the barque's existence as *Horst Wessel*; others crossed the Atlantic with the Skipper to bring *Eagle* to her new home. They are joined by members of today's German Navy, aboard, I'm told, to make certain these old sailors don't get out of line. *Could the Skipper have imagined . . . ?*

From a reunited Germany, which in the Skipper's time had been divided into East and West, we will sail on to Russia, an independent country once again, but a part of the Soviet Union when the Skipper made his voyage. There, we will represent our President and country at a celebration of the 300th anniversary of the Russian Navy. On our return trip, we will attempt to duplicate the Skipper's first *Eagle* voyage, to commemorate the 50th anniversary of bringing the barque to the United States. At the same time, we will complete the 49th consecutive cadet training cruise. *Could the Skipper have imagined . . . ?*

At times, I can hardly imagine these events, or at least my part as one of the players. It is a summer of special events in *Eagle*'s history, and I have a front row seat. I assumed command three days before sailing on this four-month voyage. With the knowledge that I would be returning to Germany with *Eagle* for the anniversary celebration, I asked my predecessor if a copy of *The Skipper and the Eagle* could be found on board in order to refresh my memory of the barque's history as we crossed the Atlantic. Having been assured that a copy was on board, I was disappointed when I was unable to find it; but, while I was still concerned over the need to be historically accurate while speaking with the press and others during our visits, I would do my best with the history that could be found in other sources on board. I resolved to search the used-book stores on our return to the States in order to restore a copy to our ship's library, but I still felt a sense of sadness that the thoughts and words of *Eagle*'s first Skipper would not be fresh in my mind as I attempted to duplicate his crossing of 50 years earlier.

Our itinerary called for two port visits, Dublin and Amsterdam, before proceeding to Hamburg. It was during a diplomatic reception in Dublin that I met the captain of the *Granuaile*, Ireland's sole buoy tender. Brendan Forde and I struck it off well right from the start, I suspect, in part, due to my background as a buoy tender sailor. On the other hand, it might have been the Boston ale that we served during our reception or the attractive young Irish-American woman cadet that seemed to put a twinkle in his eye. In either case, he confessed to me, "Captain, I've dreamed for years o' visitin' this ship . . . ever since I read *The Skipper and the Eagle*." He continued, "You'd be doin' me a great honor if you would autograph my copy of the book."

After getting over the astonishment of my first request for

an autograph, I may have caused some concern when I declared, "You have a copy of the book?! I've been dying to read the book before I get to Germany. Do you think I might borrow your copy during our port visit?" Captain Forde seemed to be having second thoughts when he inquired, "So you're not havin' a copy on board o' your own? Perhaps I'm thinkin' again o' my plan to bring the book over here!"

Brendan didn't visit *Eagle* again during our stay in Dublin, but he did rendezvous with us during our transit to the Irish Sea, bringing *Granuaile* within hailing distance so he could tell me that he would keep an eye out for a copy of *The Skipper and the Eagle*, and that some day I might find one in the mail. I still get a letter from time to time from Brendan, informing me that the search continues.

In Amsterdam, we were joined by a group of passengers who would accompany us on our transit to Hamburg, among them Holly Hollins, an editor of the magazine *Tall Ship News*, and Howard Slotnick, an organizer of Operation Sail events and a man who during my tour in *Eagle* I would come to value as a business manager, political advisor, and, most important, my friend.

As I related my story of dealing with Brendan and my search for a copy of the Skipper's book, Holly came up with an immediate solution, by reaching into her handbag, pulling out "the book" and offering, "Would you care to read my copy?" Howard, always the entrepreneur, came up with a long-term solution: "You know, it's a great story, and a shame that you can't buy the book any longer. If there's that much interest, we really ought to get it reprinted!" The seeds of a project were planted. (Note: On our return to New London that summer, Howard presented *Eagle* with a copy of "the book" that he had found in a used-book store. At the first used-book store that I visited, I found seven people on the waiting list for a copy of *The Skipper and the Eagle*.)

I'm not certain that the Skipper could have imagined that

anyone would be interested in his book nearly 40 years later, much less anyone taking on the task of reprinting it. But in his simple effort to document a small portion of *Eagle*'s history, he related a story of courage, initiative, humility and devotion to duty which stands the test of time, and should serve as both a lesson and example for the young public servants that the Coast Guard Academy strives to develop.

Could the Skipper have imagined the defining experience of cadet development? I think he certainly could have imagined and recognized *Eagle*'s large part in developing our future officers. Even in 1946 the Coast Guard recognized that sailing *Eagle* offered a cost-effective method for giving cadets an experience that would be impossible to duplicate in contemporary Coast Guard cutters. But today, even the corporate world has caught on to the need for team-building, self-confidence-developing experiences, the most recent fad being the use of former America's Cup yachts for bringing together management teams. But sail training is not a trend or fad for the Coast Guard Academy. Our Academy was started over 120 years ago aboard the schooner *J. C. Dobbin*, and sailing has been integral to our training program ever since.

But sailing only provides the venue for learning. The "*Eagle* experience," as I term it, is summed up in the motto on our ship's crest: "Tradition . . . Seamanship . . . Character."

Substitute "entry level skills" for seamanship, and I think you have a suitable motto for any profession. But we must always keep in mind that we are not training our cadets simply for a job, we are preparing them for a profession and to become career officers. In order to understand their profession, first they must know their service's history, roots, customs and heritage: Tradition. Second, we must give them the baseline skills to prepare them for their entry-level assignments: Seamanship. Finally, we must convince them to embrace the work ethic and the core values of the service and instill in them a sense of duty: Character.

218

Regarding tradition, the Academy mission states that we will graduate young men and women "with a liking for the sea and its lore." Holy-stoning decks and making baggy-wrinkle are not always popular with our young cadets, but all who sail in a square rigger come away with a greater appreciation for our country's nautical heritage. In an age of rapid technological change which is redefining the practice of navigation and seamanship, *Eagle* reminds us that seafaring is an ancient and honorable profession.

And about seamanship, we not only teach the ancient and honorable methods, we also teach the skills of today's fleet. At any time, on any day, we will have cadets undergoing damage control training by actually getting into the gear and fighting realistic simulated fires and flooding. Meanwhile, others may be occupied tracing systems in the engine room, making a boat ready for lowering, plotting a fix while transiting the coast, or taking care of the day-to-day support activities of mess cook and scullery duties.

Eagle has the basic electronic capabilities and engineering systems of contemporary Coast Guard cutters, and continued upgrades of the radar, communications gear, and electronic charting systems will help us mesh modern technology with time-tested basic seamanship skills.

And regarding character, a person learns a lot about him- or herself aboard *Eagle*, often being pushed to levels higher than the cadet may have thought possible. One boatswain of mine was fond of saying: "Any time spent in the rigging is quality time for building character." I believe courage is the first building block of character. There are few better methods for developing courage than furling the royal in the middle of the night, 140 feet above the water with wind and rain blinding you. *Eagle* and the sea present the cadets with real problems and challenges they can't walk away from. But in building a leader of character, we must first carve out a follower of character, with the proper work ethic and values.

In this regard, *Eagle* offers a tremendous leadership laboratory, with the cadets running the entire show under the supervision of the officers and crew, learning the value of teamwork, self-sacrifice, and the Coast Guard's core values of honor, respect, and devotion to duty.

Eagle is a platform where all the Academy's teachings come together. Math, chemistry, physics, history, management and other studies get practical application while the cadets perform their duties. Meanwhile, the officers who teach these subjects are brought together, complementing our wardroom each summer, because they are committed to giving our cadets a quality education, both afloat and in the classroom. While these temporary duty officers improve the cost-effectiveness of our program, they also enhance their own credibility in the classroom by demonstrating competence in their professional environment. Likewise, we augment our small year-round crew of 30 with 25 or so Coast Guard enlisted people coming from the ranks of our active, reserve, and auxiliary members. The cadets meet a great cross section of the Coast Guard family.

Tradition, seamanship, character. I would add one more informal word to that motto—fun! But while we can tell the cadets about the first three words, we can't tell them that they're going to have fun. All we can do is work hard to create the environment, by making special occasions of our personal and professional accomplishments, great port visits, taking an afternoon off for a swim call, or just enjoying the pure excitement of making 15 knots under full sail. But most of all, by ensuring that every officer, chief petty officer, and petty officer is genuinely dedicated to demonstrating the positive attitude, enthusiasm, satisfaction and joy that comes from meeting the challenges of a career at sea.

Could the Skipper have imagined . . . a national treasure? I think the aspect that the Skipper could not have imagined in his time is *Eagle*'s immense value to the United States as a very effective diplomatic and public relations tool, and her role as a very visible symbol of our country's maritime heritage. One of the benefits of *Eagle*, or of any of the world's great tall ships for that matter, is that they draw people together in a very non-threatening environment. Statesmen, diplomats, mayors, governors, industrialists, military officials or regular folks are entertained on board with dignity, respect and courtesy, and they are left with a very favorable impression of *Eagle*, the US Coast Guard, and the United States of America.

With very little notice, we can turn *Eagle* into a floating diplomatic reception hall, with cooks who can make the switch from producing 700 meals a day to dressing up for world-class parties ranging from an intimate dinner in the cabin to a formal reception for up to 300 guests.

The summer of 1996 saw *Eagle* fully and appropriately utilized in this regard, when our Ambassador to Germany held a Fourth of July reception for 250 people on board and our Ambassador to Russia hosted a reception for 300 people to honor the Russian Navy's anniversary. During visiting hours in Germany, we entertained 23,000 people on board, and in Russia, over 25,000. We were exposed to hundreds of thousands of people who viewed us from shoreside and millions of Europeans saw us during television coverage. What ship of war of equivalent size, or even larger, can draw that kind of favorable attention?

But 1996 was not a one-time event. *Eagle* has impressed people around the world, most notably during her mission to Australia at the direction of President Reagan, to a tall ships event to commemorate that country's bicentennial. But President Reagan was not the first to take note of *Eagle* or the inspirational value of the tall ships. President Kennedy gave his support to the first Operation Sail held in 1964 which, unfortunately, he did not live to see. *Eagle* served as the flagship for OpSail that year, just as she has for follow-up events in 1976, 1980, 1986 and 1992. Just as she stirred the hearts of millions of Americans during those events, she will surely repeat her majestic performance as she leads an even larger procession of tall ships into American ports as a part of the OpSail 2000 festivities.

Could the Skipper have imagined . . . 50 years of service? I'm not a naval engineer, but people experienced in the profession have examined *Eagle* and found her to be in sound condition. As I look around the ship, I am encouraged by the basic durability, strength of design and function. Of course, every *Eagle* captain will be concerned about the routine budgetary and personnel support to conduct proper preventive maintenance on the engineering systems, the sails and rigging, routine services and outfitting, and to maintain the quality and safety of the program.

I've had the opportunity to see many of the world's existing tall ships, and while *Eagle* is certainly one of the senior citizens of the group, she's far from the oldest. Russia's *Kruzenshtern* is 73 and *Sedov* is 77, both still training cadets and in pretty good shape in spite of the years of hard service and lack of resources in Russia. Many of the wooden sailing ships we raced with in Europe during 1996 had celebrated over 100 years. Back at home, the iron-hulled *Star of India* in San Diego is over 130 years old and still goes out under sail on special occasions. Of the *Star* Alan Villiers wrote: "When she was built. . . nobody knew how long they might be good for, and there were still skeptics who held that iron ships would not float at all. So they built them solid and they built them good. Good iron looked after may be made to last almost forever."

Eagle was built at the height of steel square rigger experience and technology, by the masters of windjammer construction, with good German steel. I believe that if she is "looked after" she may be made to last another 50 years.

I mentioned that during the summer of 1996 we would

attempt to recreate the Skipper's voyage to the United States. But we had certain advantages that did not exist in the Skipper's time—satellite navigation, worldwide communications, improved weather predictions and monitoring and a well-trained crew. We did have a case of suspected appendicitis on board and we even had a brush with a hurricane in the vicinity of Bermuda. All the modern equipment helped us avoid rather than fight the storm. But the elements of the experience are still there, and we still get enough weather to provide the environment for developing sailors—people who tend to be individuals who have known great challenges and survived, who know that no matter how bad it gets in a storm, eventually it will get better. Sailors learn that no matter how difficult the problem, no matter how severe the storm, you continue to struggle because quitting is unthinkable and often carries tragic consequences. Sailors are survivors; sailors are optimists; sailors are problem-solvers; sailors are believers; and it will take that sailor spirit to carry our Coast Guard and our country into the next century.

Eagle has developed that spirit by providing a useful, character-building experience while serving as a vital link between our past and our future, and between every Academy graduate over the past 50 years. God willing, it will be so for the *Eagle* and her people for another 50 years.

Could the Skipper have imagined . . . ?

CAPTAIN ROBERT J. PAPP, JR.
USCG Barque *Eagle*

In the Bremerhaven drydock, 1946.

Ka-Leut, the Skipper (center) and a German seaman, 1946. All photos are courtesy the US Coast Guard unless noted otherwise.

Eddie Didion, Mike Pasko, Ed Lowe, and Dave Ruley aboard *Eagle* in the chiefs' dining area aft, 1946.
Photo by Dave Ruley, courtesy Edward Lowe.

The *Eagle* sails in company with her sisters *Sagres II* and *Gorch Fock*, 1992.

The *Eagle* returned to Hamburg in June 1996, sixty years after she was launched from the Blohm & Voss Shipyard. Here former *Horst Wessel* crew tour the vessel as *Eagle* crew and cadets host a reception aboard.

Captain Papp, second from left, hosts former *Horst Wessel* sailors in *Eagle*'s cabin, June 1996.

Youth groups are frequent visitors to the *Eagle*. Here a cadet demonstrates steering to a Scout group, using both the old triple wheel the ship has had since 1936 and the new electronic equipment.

On a visit while the ship is in Miami, youngsters are shown a life vest and the emergency equipment that comes with it.

A Note on Names and People

This is a list of *Eagle* personnel as of the day of commissioning, 22 May 1946. The *Eagle* sailed on 30 May and some listed here may not have remained aboard for the voyage.

US Coast Guard Crew

Cmdr. G.P. McGowan
Lt. Cmdr. R.M. Hutchins
Lt. Cmdr. R.S. Von Burske ("Von")
Lt. F.A. Goettel
Lt. F.P. Jascak
Lt. O.C. Woodruff
Lt.(jg) J.C. Macfarlane

Andersen, Gunner E., SC1c
Babich, Emil S., MoMM2c
Bagwell, Eugene C., CMoMM
Barnes, Henry G., Jr., S2c
Bergmark, Karl E., S2c
Billings, Marlin G., S2c
Bishop, W.M., S1c
Bodine, William H., BM1c
Bowden, Henry G., Jr., MoMM1c
Buckley, John J., S2c
Burrows, Ambrose H., S2c
Butler, John P., F2c
Cardenas, Gilbert, S2c
Carmody, Daniel, F2c
Champoux, Joseph, S2c
Chisum, Grady, S2c
Chovan, Frank, S2c
Clay, John M., S2c
Damato, Andrea, BM2c
Davis, Edward D., S2c
De Bernardi, James F., S1c
Delainedis, Theodore, S1c
Dyer, Joseph E., S2c
Glowski, Jerome, RM1c
Goins, Earl V., SC1c
Gotwols, Edwin P., S1c
Hinson, Pete M., CM1c
Honer, Richard P., StM1c

Jones, Edward I., S2c
Kilna, Joseph R., S2c
Kromberg, Jos. J., MoMM2c
Lindstrom, Carl E., S2c
Lowe, Edward T., CEM
Lyon, David M., S1c
McNaughton, E.K., S2c
Meyers, R.F., BM1c
Morris, Carlos C., S1c
Nacarelli, Albert F., S2c
Noehren, Henry P., MoMM2c
Olikshinski, Charles, RM1c
Olsen, John H., BM1c
Pasko, Michael W., CBM
Phillips, Alfred H., QM1c
Poe, Earl L., S2c
Reynaud, Eugene, RM3c
Ruley, David T., CPhoM*
Schlapinski, Robert, S2c
Smith, William N., S2c
Terrels, Joseph, RM3c
Testa, Serafino, QM3c
Tuck, Paul C., RM3c
Wallace, Ray V., S2c
Watson, Daniel M., S2c
Westcott, Richard N., S1c
White, Luther, StM2c

* *David Ruley took most of the photos of the 1946 voyage.*

German Crew

Kapitänleutnant Barthold Schnibbe
Leutnant zur See Hugo Schreyer
Sanitäts Oberfähnrich Ernst Losehner
Bootsmann Erich Schultz
Obermaschinist Heinrich Ress
Feldwebel Rudi Schwalm
Oberbootsmaat Wilhelm Bottcher
Oberbootsmaat Gerhard Brunne
Oberbootsmaat Werner L'Orange

Becker, Bernhard	Laderick, Kurt
Bodecker, Harald	Machon, Christian
Bohde, Hans U.	Mandel, Roland
Buchta, Georg	Matther, Lothar
Christiansen, Gerd	Mau, Ulf Gunther
Deubner, Roland	Meister, Hermann
Dombrowski, Leo	Murswick, Guenter
Drews, Gerd	Nisch, Ludwig
Dunkel, Bruno	Scheder, Bieschim
Fahl, Gunther	Schmidt, Helmut
Fahrion, Hermann	Schroder, Rolf
Haeger, Hans J.	Schroder, Reinhard
Harbeck, Gerd	Schutte, Heino
Hartman, Werner	Soboll, Walter
Helmenstein, Siegfried	Starek, Willi
Jepsen, Herger	Stein, Siegfried
Krenzin, Heinz	Stiebel, Gerhard
Krenzler, Hans J.	Stuhmer, Jeny
Kueherzke, Emil	Valentin, Bernd
Kuhnke, Heins	Winkler, Heins

"Ducky," the resourceful American naval reserve officer, is Everard C. Endt, well-known yacht-racing helmsman who, like so many yachtsmen, had joined the US Navy "for the duration."

The Danish officer who made the trip at McGowan's invitation was Knud Langvard, former executive officer of the *Danmark*.

According to a contemporary news account on the "Mystery Boy" of Bremerhaven, Eddie Didion was orphaned in Normandy and was cared for by a US Army MP battalion. When that unit went home, he found shelter at the US Navy Weser River Patrol Base. He was 14 when the *Eagle* crew took him in. Small for his age and a hard worker, he earned the affection of US servicemen. His fate remains unknown.

230

Commanding Officers of
USCG Barque Eagle, *1946 to 1999*

#1	Captain Gordon P. McGowan	1946–47
#2	Captain Miles H. Imlay	1947–48
#3	Captain Carl B. Olsen	1949–50
#4	Captain Carl G. Bowman	1950–54
#5	Captain Karl O. A. Zittel	1955–57
#6	Captain William B. Ellis	1958–59
#7	Captain Chester I. Steele	1960–61
#8	Captain Robert A. Schulz	1961–62
#9	Captain William K. Earle	1963–65
#10	Captain Archibald B. How	1965–66
#11	Captain Stephen G. Carkeek	1966–68
#12	Commander Harold A. Paulsen	1968–70
#13	Captain Edward D. Cassidy	1970–73
#14	Captain James C. Irwin	1974–75
#15	Captain James R. Kelly	1975–76
#16	Captain Paul E. Welling	1976–80
#17	Captain Martin J. Moynihan	1980–83
#18	Captain Ernst M. Cummings	1983–88
#19	Captain David V.V. Wood	1988–92
#20	Captain Patrick M. Stillman	1992–95
#21	Captain Donald R. Grosse	1995–96
#22	Captain Robert J. Papp, Jr.	1996–99

Itinerary of USCG Barque Eagle, *1946 to 1998*

1946 Martha's Vineyard / Nantucket / New Bedford (all in Massachusetts)

1947 Bermuda / Caneel Bay, Virgin Islands / San Juan, PR / Nassau, Bahamas / Miami, FL / Coral Gables, FL / Parris Island, SC / Norfolk, VA / New York, NY

1948 Ponta Delgada, Azores / London, England / Le Havre, France / Santa Cruz, Canary Islands / Bermuda

1949 London, England / Antwerp, Belgium / Lisbon, Portugal / Casablanca, Morocco / Santa Cruz, Canary Islands

1950 Amsterdam, Netherlands / Antwerp, Belgium / Lisbon, Portugal / Funchal, Madeira

1951 London and Portsmouth, England / Antwerp, Belgium / Amsterdam, Netherlands / Le Havre, France / Lisbon, Portugal /Casablanca, Morocco / Canary Islands / Halifax, NS / Bermuda

1952 Oslo, Norway / Copenhagen, Denmark / Santander, Spain / Las Palmas, Canary Islands

1953 Oslo, Norway / Antwerp, Belgium / Santander, Spain / Las Palmas, Canary Islands

1954 Santander, Spain / Amsterdam, Netherlands / Copenhagen, Denmark / Bermuda

1955 Glasgow, Scotland / Le Havre, France / Lisbon, Portugal / Le Havre, France / Lisbon, Portugal / Madeira / Bermuda

1956 San Juan, PR / Coco Solo, Panama Canal Zone / Havana, Cuba / Halifax, NS

1957 Bergen, Norway / London, England / La Coruna, Spain

1958 Amsterdam, Netherlands / Dublin, Ireland / Lisbon, Portugal / Madeira / Bermuda

1959 San Juan, PR / Ciudad Trujillo, Dominican Rep. / Willemstad, Curaçao / Kingston, Jamaica / Gardiners Bay, NY / Quebec City, QC / Nantucket and Provincetown, MA

1960 Oslo, Norway / Portsmouth, England / Le Havre, France

1961 Bordeaux, France / Lisbon, Portugal / Cadiz, Spain / Santa Cruz de Tenerife, Canary Islands

1962 Edinburgh, Scotland / Antwerp, Belgium / Las Palmas, Canary Islands / Washington, DC / Yorktown, VA

1963 Oslo, Norway / Amsterdam, Netherlands / Santander, Spain / Funchal, Madeira

1964 San Juan, PR / Bermuda / New York, NY / Quebec City, QC / Bermuda

1965 Miami, FL / Panama City, Panama / Acapulco, Mexico / Long Beach, CA / Seattle, WA / San Francisco, CA / San Diego, CA

1966 Wilmington, NC / Boston, MA

1967 Montreal, Quebec / Cape May, NJ / Providence, RI / Nantucket, MA

1968 New York, NY / Provincetown, MA / Portsmouth, NH / Yorktown, VA / Hamilton, Bermuda

1969 Norfolk, VA / New York, NY/ Portland, ME / Newport, RI

1970 Southport, NC / Portsmouth, VA / New York, NY / Newport, RI

1971 St. George, Bermuda / Boston, MA / Portsmouth, NH / Newburyport, MA

1972 Mobile, AL / New Orleans, LA / Galveston, TX / Portsmouth, England / Lübeck, W. Germany / Lisbon, Portugal / Madeira

1973 Boston, MA / San Juan, PR / Port Everglades, FL / Charleston, SC / New Bedford, MA / Newburyport, MA / Philadelphia, PA

1974 Washington, DC / St. George, Bermuda / Newport, RI / Boston, MA / New York, NY / Portsmouth, NH / New Bedford, MA

1975 Antwerp, Belgium / Le Havre, France / Rota, Spain / Malaga, Spain / Funchal, Madeira

1976 Philadelphia, PA / Alexandria, VA / Bermuda / Newport, RI / New York, NY / Baltimore, MD / Jacksonville, FL / Miami, FL / Charleston, SC / New Bedford, MA

1977 Hamburg, West Germany / London, England / Rota, Spain

1978 Guantanamo, Cuba / Cristobal, Panama / Acapulco, Mexico / San Diego, CA / Victoria, BC / Seattle, WA / San Francisco, CA / Long Beach, CA

1979 Halifax, NS / Norfolk, VA / Washington, DC / New York, NY

/ Bermuda / Savannah, GA

1980 Boston, MA / St. Thomas, VI / San Juan, PR / Barbados / St. Lucia / Santo Domingo, Dominican Republic / St. Petersburg, FL / Miami, FL / Charleston, SC

1981 Cork, Ireland / Lisbon, Portugal / Rota, Spain / Malaga, Spain / Las Palmas, Canary Islands / Bermuda / New Haven, CT

1982 Washington, DC / Norfolk, VA / Philadelphia, PA / Newport, RI / New York, NY / Portland, ME

1983 Port of Spain, Trinidad / St. Thomas, VI / Roosevelt Roads, PR / Port Everglades, FL / Bermuda

1984 New Orleans, LA / Halifax, NS / Quebec City, Quebec / Portsmouth, NH / Bourne, MA

1985 Cape Canaveral, FL / Mobile, AL / Jacksonville, FL / Bermuda / Boston, MA / St. Pierre et Miquelon / New Bedford, MA / Gloucester, MA

1986 Yorktown, VA / Hamilton, Bermuda / Washington, DC / Hamilton, Bermuda / Norfolk, VA / New York, NY / Halifax, NS / Newport, RI / Portland, ME / Portsmouth, NH

1987 New York, NY / New London, CT / Fall River, MA / New Bedford, MA / Palm Beach, FL / Rodman, Panama / Guyaquil, Ecuador / Galapagos, Ecuador / Papeete, Tahiti / Bora Bora / Society Islands / Pago Pago, American Samoa / Apia, Western Samoa / Nukualofa, Tonga / Vavau, Tonga / New Castle, Australia / Brisbane, Australia

1988 Hobart, Tasmania / Sydney, Australia / Manly, Australia / Pago Pago, American Samoa / Honolulu, HI / Seattle, WA / San Francisco, CA / Long Beach, CA / Acapulco, Mexico / Rodman, Panama / Miami, FL / Edinburgh, Scotland / Bergen, Norway / Hamburg, W. Germany / Antwerp, Belgium / Santa Cruz, Canary Islands / Bermuda

1989 New York, NY / London, England / Cork, Ireland / Leningrad, USSR / Aalborg, Denmark / Horseus, Denmark / Helsinki, Finland / Roven, France / Horta, Azores / Halifax, NS / Portland, ME / Washington, DC / Savannah, GA / Yorktown, VA

1990 Tampa, FL / Mobile, AL / New Orleans, LA / Wilmington, NC / Washington, DC / Norfolk, VA / Portsmouth, VA /

Charleston, SC / New York, NY / Boothbay Harbor, ME / Boston, MA / Kennebunkport, ME / Philadelphia, PA / Baltimore, MD / Fall River, MA / Newport, RI / Portsmouth, NH / Halifax, NS

1991 Yorktown, VA / Ponta Delgada, Azores / Cherbourg, France / Weymouth, England / Lisbon, Portugal / Funchal, Madeira / Bermuda / Gloucester, MA / Washington, DC

1992 Roosevelt Roads, PR / San Juan, PR / Nassau, Bahamas / New York, NY / Boston, MA / Newport, RI / Portland, ME / Norfolk, VA / Morehead City, NC / Savannah, GA

1993 Dublin, Ireland / Oporto, Portugal / Cadiz, Spain / Funchal, Madeira / Bermuda / New London, CT

1994 Baltimore, MD / Washington, DC / Ponta Delgada, Azores / Plymouth, England / Rouen, France / Bermuda / Newport, RI / New London, CT

1995 New York, NY / Norfolk, VA / New London, CT / New Haven, CT / Portsmouth, NH / Halifax, NS / Louisbourg, NS / Fall River, MA / New London, CT

1996 Dublin, Ireland / Amsterdam, Netherlands / Hamburg, Germany / Rostock, Germany / St. Petersburg, Russia / Helsinki, Finland / London, England / Portsmouth, England / Ponta Delgada, Azores / Bermuda

1997 Plymouth, England / Copenhagen, Denmark / Den Helder, Netherlands / Bermuda / Norfolk, VA

1998 (Winter Cruise) Roosevelt Roads, PR / Martinique, French Antilles / La Guaira, Venezuela / Cartagena, Colombia (Summer Cruise) New York, NY / Washington, DC / San Juan, PR / Miami, FL / Savannah, GA / Boston, MA / Halifax, NS / Portland, ME

Kapitänleutnant Schnibbe's Report

After the voyage Ka-Leut issued the following report to his superiors in Germany.

Report of Crossing of U.S.C.G.C. *Eagle*
(ex S.S.S. *Horst Wessel*)

After the successful commissioning by the U.S. Coast Guard on 22 May 1946 and the final trip preparations, the U.S.C. G. C. *Eagle* (ex S.S.S. *Horst Wessel*) departed from Bremerhaven on 30 May 1946 at 1000 hours. The ship proceeded at first under its own power and was then on 31 May 1946 taken in tow by the High Seas Tug *Passat*, which was to accompany the ship to Falmouth/England. In spite of the sometimes rough seas the passage through the Channel took place without any special incidents. The tug *Passat* did splendid work, which was acknowledged also by the ship's American management and by the two British officers aboard for the trip to Falmouth. The ship reached Falmouth during the evening of 2 June and dropped anchor in Falmouth roads. As the weather conditions were particularly unfavorable, it was decided to await better weather and to take on oil.

On 6 June 1946 the ship left Falmouth, setting course for Funchal/Madeira. At first the ship proceeded under power, and the tug was discharged back to Germany. When the breeze picked up, sails were set and all maneuvers were executed by the three watches made up of the two crews. At the same time classes were scheduled, as the German crew members had to learn the American commands, and the American crew had to learn the sense of the sailing maneu-

236

vers. During this training the main royal was lost, as the salvage of this older sail could not be completed quickly enough because of the increasing winds. On 9 June 1946 Porto Santo came into sight, and at about 2400 hours the ship dropped anchor in Funchal roads; there as in other ports the German crew could not go ashore because of the political situation and because no peace treaty had been signed. After taking on water and oil, the ship continued the voyage on 14 June. Course was set so far south, that the ship could utilize the prevailing Passat winds, and as a result she ran most of the way to Bermuda under sail. During this part of the voyage, in addition to the seamanship training, much attention was given to putting the ship in order and painting it.

On 30 June the ship reached Bermuda and anchored in the harbor of Fort Hamilton. In addition to replacing consumables, the ship's attention focused on the preparations for the inspection by Rear Admiral Peine, U.S.C.G., and the British Governor. The muster by the Rear Admiral, who was also on board for the departure on 5 July and some sailing exercises at sea, proceeded to his full satisfaction, as the Admiral indicated also to the German Commandant repeatedly. During the evening of 6 July the weather suddenly deteriorated dramatically and developed into a hurricane which reached its high point during the afternoon of 7 July so that the ship was forced to turn into the wind and four older square sails were lost. At times the wind reached speeds of 65 miles per hour, and it is notable that the ship for several minutes was listing at 45 degrees. In spite of all this, no sailor on board experienced a sense of danger, the ship conducted herself quite admirably. During the night of 8 July the weather cleared except for a few squalls from the west, and by morning the winds had died down altogether. After some necessary repairs and removal of some damaged sails the Ambrose lightship was reached the same day at 1700 hours and at about 2100 hours anchor was dropped in New York harbor.

In accordance with orders received by telegraph the ship proceeded the next day up the Hudson and stopped after about 20 miles at the pier of Camp Shanks. Here the German crew was shipped out and taken to Camp Shanks. In the camp the crew was at first kept isolated from the German POWs, but after receipt of instructions from Washington, which the Camp commandant had requested, the crew was taken into the POW camp. Here they were registered, dressed in POW uniforms and assigned POW numbers. The MDG uniforms as well as all naval gear of the crew were stored for them and later on reissued on the transport. In the camp as well as on board the two transports the crew was treated correctly, but on the other hand, in accordance with instructions from Washington, was given no opportunity to get in touch with relatives or friends.

Together with the last German POWs in the USA, the crew was put on board the *Elgin Victory* in New York on 21 July 1946; the ship was destined for Le Havre and then Italy. The voyage went without incidents, worth noting is the understanding which was shown by the transport officer as well as by the naval officers on board; the naval officers especially were very interested in details of the training ship which had crossed the Atlantic. On 31 July 1946 Le Havre was reached and the transport officer arranged that the crew could remain in their MDG uniforms on board the *Elgin Victory* until the next morning when the *Texarcana Victory* entered port in order to proceed from Le Havre to Bremerhaven. The American Command in Le Havre agreed to let the German crew change to the *Texarcana Victory*, so that the crew arrived in Bremerhaven on 3 August 1946, where they were welcomed by Commander Lord of the U.S. Navy and the representative of the S.G.N.O. (B). An 18-day furlough, to start the next day, concluded this crossing.

238

In conclusion it is worth mentioning that during the crossing to the USA there were no incidents between the two crews, the cooperation was good, by order of the Commandant food and issuance of canteen goods were the same for the German as for the American crew, so that in these two critical areas there was no cause for friction. The ship itself showed excellent qualities during all sorts of weather and never allowed a feeling of insecurity to arise.

Signed: Schnibbe
Kapitänleutnant
Former Commandant of the
Sailing School Ship *Horst Wessel*